When Did I See You Hungry?

Written and Photographed by
Gerard Thomas Straub

ST. ANTHONY MESSENGER PRESS
Cincinnati, Ohio

Credits

Scripture citations are taken from *The New Revised Standard Version Bible*, copyright ©1989 by the Division of Christian Education of the National Council of Churches of Christ in the United States of America, and used by permission. All rights reserved.

The source for statistics on hunger and poverty in this book is Bread for the World.

The photograph on page 175 is used by permission of Vincent Reyes, O.F.M. CAP.

Excerpts from Mother Teresa's *The Joy in Loving: A Guide to Daily Living with Mother Teresa*, copyright ©2000, used by permission of Viking Press, a division of Penguin Putnam, Inc.

Excerpts from Thomas Merton's *No Man Is an Island*, copyright ©1955, used by permission of Harcourt, Inc.

Excerpts from Dom Helder Camara's *Hoping Against All Hope*, copyright ©1994, used by permission of Orbis Books.

"Fr. Mychal's Prayer," by Fr. Mychal Judge, O.F.M., Chaplain, New York Fire Department, copyright ©2001 by Holy Name Province, used by permission of Holy Name Province.

Cover and interior design by Sandy L. Digman
Photographs by Gerard Thomas Straub

ISBN 0-86716-502-2
Copyright ©2002, Gerard Thomas Straub

All rights reserved.
Published by St. Anthony Messenger Press
www.AmericanCatholic.org
Printed in the U.S.A.

Library of Congress Cataloging-in-Publication Data

Straub, Gerard Thomas, 1947-
 When did I see you hungry? / written and photographed by Gerard Thomas Straub.
  p. cm.
 ISBN 0-86716-502-2 (hardcover)
 1. Portrait photography. 2. Poor—Developing countries—Portraits.
 3. Hunger in art. 4. Poverty—Religious aspects. 5. Hunger—Religious aspects. I. Title.
 TR681.P6 S87 2002
 362.5'022'2—dc21

                              2002009391

Manila, the Philippines

In memoriam

Teresa Marie Hettenbach

my younger sister who entered the fullness
of God on April 21, 2002. Her far
too brief life reflected God's love in
countless acts of kindness. ℬ

This book is dedicated to **Michael Duffy, O.F.M.**
and **Francis Pompei, O.F.M.,** _with gratitude_
for teaching me to see the poor as my
brothers and sisters.

With special thanks to
Monsignor Richard Albert
Bienvenido Q. Baisas, O.F.M.
Tony Barsamian
David Beckmann
Larry Bernard, O.F.M.
Joel Bernardo, C.M.
Lisa Biedenbach
Giacomo Bini, O.F.M.
Murray Bodo, O.F.M.
April Bolton
Barry Brown, O.F.M. CAP.
Betty Campbell, R.S.M.
Julius Canonoy, O.F.M.

Friedrick Chudalla, O.F.M.
Sean Collins, O.F.M.
Vincent Cushing, O.F.M.
Sandy Digman
Trevor D'Souza, O.F.M.
Ed Dunn, O.F.M.
Rocky Evangelista, S.D.B.
James B. Flickinger, S.F.M.
Daniel Fox, O.F.M. CAP.
Reu Jose Galoy, O.F.M.
Felix Gassam, O.F.M.
Brian Thomas Gerhard
Peter Hinde, O. CARM.
Juan Maria Huerta, O.F.M.
Carol Kane, F.M.M.
Michael Kellett, O.F.M.
Daniel Lackie, O.F.M.
John Lafferty
John Lange, M.M.
Celso Larracas, O.F.M.
Jomar B. Legaspi, S.D.B.
Srimanie Leitan, F.M.M.
Paul Long
Tisha Lozano
Jenny Lukacovic
Robert Manansala, O.F.M.
Finian McGinn, O.F.M.
Hugh McKenna, O.F.M.
Jonathan Montaldo
Dominic Monti, O.F.M.
Gregory R. Morris
Juan Ignacio Muro, O.F.M.
Patti and Ray Normile

Vic Onting, S.D.B.
Samuel Lopez Padilla, O.F.M.
Roly Pimentero, O.F.M.
Paul Quenon, O.C.S.O.
Reginald A. Redlon, O.F.M.
Vincent Reyes, O.F.M. CAP.
Igor Ridanović
Richard Rohr, O.F.M.
Rick Samyn, O.F.M. CAP.
Robert L. Schmidt
Robert Smith, S.F.M.
Mark Soehner, O.F.M.
Ray Stadmeyer, O.F.M. CAP.
Joseph J. Straub
Kathleen M. Straub
Dexter Rey T. Sumaoy, O.F.M.
Arock Sunder, O.F.M.
Rose Tcheza, F.M.M.
Patrick Toya
Ulic Troy, O.F.M.
Nancyann Turner, O.P.
Louis Vitale, O.F.M.
Mary Williamson, F.M.M.
Francis Wendling, O.F.M.
Grace Yap, O.S.F.
for their help in making this book a reality.

And an extra special thanks to
Gearóid Francisco Ó Conaire, O.F.M.
whose inspiration and help were beyond measure.

In the economy of divine charity we have only as much as we give. But we are called upon to give as much as we have, and more: as much as we are. So the measure of our love is theoretically without limit. The more we desire to give ourselves in charity, the more charity we will have to give. And the more we give the more truly we shall be. For the Lord endows us with a being proportionate to the giving for which we are destined.

—THOMAS MERTON, *No Man Is an Island*

Rome, Italy

Table of Contents

We learn to see the face of Christ—the face of Christ that is also the face of a suffering human being, the face of the crucified, the face of the poor, the face of the saint, and the face of every person—and we love each one with the criteria with which we will be judged: "I was hungry and you gave me to eat."

—ARCHBISHOP OSCAR ROMERO, quoted in
Oscar Romero: Reflections on His Life and Writings
by Marie Dennis, Renny Golden, Scott Wright

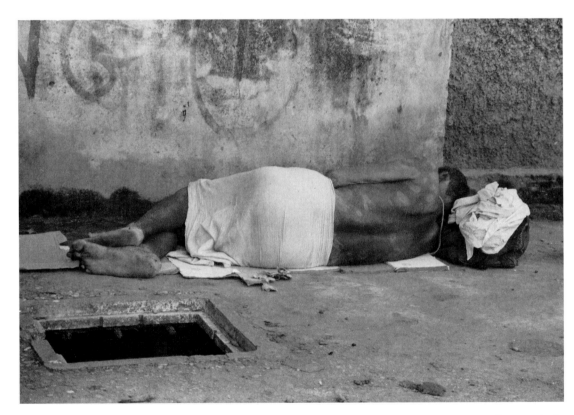

Chennai, India

"When I walk with Jesus, He always leads me to the poorest, the lowliest and the lost, so that I may open my heart to them." —JEAN VANIER

hy is a Hollywood television producer taking photographs in the slums of India, Kenya, Brazil, Jamaica, Mexico and the Philippines? I'm not sure—and I am the television producer in question. Oddly enough, it was a long-dead saint from medieval Italy who drew me to the horrific slums where countless people live in cruel, painful poverty.

Before the year 1995, I had never given the subject of poverty much thought. I had felt a sense of compassion toward the poor and made some minimal donations to a handful of charitable organizations. But I was more concerned with avoiding poverty than understanding it. Poverty was something from which to flee and certainly not something one would deliberately embrace. I chased after Brother Porsche.

In March of 1995, during a trip to Italy to research a novel I was writing, I encountered a saint who made poverty a way of life—Saint Francis of Assisi. Despite my being an atheist at the time, Francis captivated my heart and mind; the powerful story of his life, with its unconditional and unrestricted response to God, turned my life upside down. I abandoned the novel and devoted the next four years of my life to writing about him and his friend, Saint Clare of Assisi. While writing *The Sun and Moon Over Assisi*, I had to face head on Francis' undying devotion to poverty, which he took for his bride, and grapple with the relevancy it had for the world today. I was also graced with the opportunity to see the saint's ideals being lived by Franciscan friars and sisters who feed five hundred people a day in the slums of Philadelphia. Living in the slums with the friars while making a documentary film on their work with the poor, *We Have a Table for Four Ready*, forever changed my view of the poor and helped me begin to understand Saint Francis' romance with poverty.

In the fall of 1999, after delivering the final draft of my book to the publisher, I was faced with a huge void in my life. For four years, *The Sun and Moon Over Assisi* was the focal point of my existence. And now it was finished. While writing the book, my life was slowly being transformed, my faith fully restored. Among other spiritual lessons, Saint Francis had shown me how to see the face of Christ in the poor. How to live the medieval saint's ideal of poverty as a modern, secular person became my main challenge in life. Seeing Christ in the poor is laudable, but you are left with figuring out what to do, how to respond. I decided to enter the bloated belly of poverty in order to learn how to respond to the poor, the weak, the suffering and the marginalized whose ranks swell with each passing year. I spent months living among the poor of San

Francisco, Los Angeles, Albuquerque, Philadelphia, Detroit (United States); Toronto (Canada); Rome (Italy); Nairobi, Wang'uru (Kenya); Manaus (Brazil); Calcutta, Guwahati, Rangjuli, Bangalore, Chennai (India); Juarez, San Quintin, Tijuana (Mexico); Manila (the Philippines) and Kingston (Jamaica). I listened to their stories, and to the stories of the men and women who have dedicated their lives to offering the poor some relief, some ray of hope. Armed only with a pen and a 35-mm camera, I entered the bleak world of unimaginable poverty in order to help shed some light on this dark corner of humanity.

This book is about poverty and our responsibility to help those who are forced to live in poverty. The photographs in this book depict real people—suffering souls whose lives are spent in the cruel prison of poverty. To look into their eyes, eyes that are profoundly human and tragically sad, compels the observer to want to do something to relieve the misery. Figuring out what to do is a major problem. But there is one person who lived and died two thousand years ago who seemed to know clearly what we should do, and this book tells us what he said...even though his advice is hard to follow. Very hard.

In these pages, the reader will often come across a familiar name: Jesus. Jesus plays a part in this story because he hung out with the poor, and he always sided with the poor, preferring their company to the more well-to-do of his society. Jesus, we so easily forget, was born in a food trough used to feed oxen. Jesus knew and lived poverty.

Despite the recent increase in secularism, the majority of people in the Americas, Europe and Oceania are Christians. As such, they try to follow the teachings of Jesus, albeit with varying degrees of intensity and sincerity. Yet when it comes to the poor, most Christians ignore the example and directions of Christ. I know I did so for most of my life. And still do so.

Recently, thanks to the inspiration of Saint Francis of Assisi, I reconnected to the Christian faith I had abandoned decades ago. Today, I see myself as a sinner struggling with my own human frailty, my own spiritual poverty. As I began to follow Christ again, I was led to the margins of society and introduced to the poorest of the poor, to Christ's best friends. This book is about them and about us and how we (Christians and non-Christians alike) respond to them, the people Jesus called "blessed" and we call "cursed."

I hope my frequent mention of Jesus does not become a roadblock that prevents non-Christians from entering the world of poverty I have captured on film. I am not an evangelist, nor am I promoting Christianity in this book. I mention Jesus simply to introduce his ideas and philosophy on poverty and the poor to Christians who seem to have forgotten Jesus' love of and preference for the poor and his instruction to care for them. In this book, I point out Jesus' relationship with the poor because I believe Christians should be striving to emulate and duplicate that relationship with the poor today. Clearly, we are—*I am*—not doing so. In addition to Jesus, the book mentions many other people, from many different faiths, who also harbored a deep love and concern for the poor in their hearts. For instance, in these pages you will hear Albert Einstein's, Mahatma Gandhi's and the Dalai Lama's thoughts on poverty and our need to help the poor.

The title *When Did I See You Hungry?* is from the New Testament. When I first heard it I wasn't in a church. I was in a litter-strewn alley behind an abandoned, burned-out building in Philadelphia, where homeless people slept and drug addicts got high. A dreadful, frightening place. I was making a film about a soup kitchen run by Franciscan friars. As I stood in the rubble of the alley on a bitterly cold day, the priest spoke about the passage in Matthew's Gospel that says on the day of the last judgment people will be separated into two camps: one will be populated by those who fed and clothed Jesus, and the other with those who did not. And the eternal outlook for those who did not is not sunny. I found the passage troubling when I first heard it and I still do.

The photographs in this book show life in slums around the world. They capture the dignity, hope, courage and joy—along with the sadness and despair—I found in those slums. Some of the photographs are tough to look at. They are, however, not meant to make you feel downcast or ashamed or guilty. I am not interested in shaming anyone into helping the poor. I simply want to show you their life, a life lived without the basic essentials we take for granted. Most of these people live without electricity or running water; most do not have an adequate supply of food or clean drinking water; they live in homes made of mud and sticks and plastic tarps or scraps of wood and metal. Their lives are riddled with an array of deadly diseases caused by malnutrition; few have access to even the most basic medical care or medicine. Blindness is common; a broken arm or even a minor cut can be fatal. Besides food, the children hunger for acceptance and affection. The

people in the slums of the Third World and on the streets of America I visited are isolated, ignored and unwanted, and they know they are seen as a blight on society. Life for the people in these photographs has been reduced to learning to live without.

The words that accompany the photographs in Part Two are also difficult. In fact, they are downright unreasonable. But they are the truth—the gospel truth. What I have learned—and it came as quite a surprise—is that Jesus is not asking us to give a few bucks from our excess; he is asking us to give our lives. The text is tough…and demanding. But it is the truth— a truth that I cannot follow or obey. *But I want to…and that is a start.*

All who pick up this book have seen Jesus hungry and hurting, whether they recognized him or not. At least once in your life—even if only in your own family—you responded, you helped, you put others before yourself. You may have wiped the tears away from your little sister's face, or shared a sandwich with your grammar school classmate, or helped a stranger who was in an accident. In this book, I am not pointing a finger at anyone and saying: "You have not done enough." I have met the people in these photographs, and I am saying, "I have not done enough; and,

moreover, I am part of the reason such unjust poverty exists." I know what God is asking me to do in response to the cries of the poor. I do not know what God is asking you to do. Only you can find that out. But no matter what you or I are doing—*God is asking each of us to do more.*

The poor are among us. Millions upon millions of them. They are hungry and naked. We need to feed and clothe them. And when we do, we are feeding and clothing Jesus…and ourselves.

It is my sincere prayer that this humble book will light a candle in the darkness and inspire some helping hearts and hands. I suggest meditating each day on just one page for five minutes…to see where it leads you. My hunch is it will lead you out of yourself, to the poor and to God.

I offer special thanks to Giacomo Bini, O.F.M., Minister General of the Order of Friars Minor, whose own words will conclude this introduction to the photographs and whose early endorsement of this project opened many doors for me, and to Gearóid Francisco Ó Conaire, O.F.M., an Irish Franciscan friar who was a missionary in El Salvador for many years, without whose help and inspiration the book could never have been completed. To both I am deeply indebted. ℘

No man who ignores the rights and needs of others can hope to walk in the light of contemplation, because his way has turned aside from truth, from compassion, and therefore from God. The obstacle is in our "self," that is to say in the tenacious need to maintain our separate, external, egocentric will.

—THOMAS MERTON,
New Seeds of Contemplation

Assisi, Italy

YOUNG FRANCIS OF ASSISI was in the rag trade—at the upper end. He fitted out the rich in exotic plumes so they need never forget that they were a different breed from the grubby unwashed in their hovels. And Francis ached to be like them, a bird of paradise.

Things, however, took a strange turn. Francis found himself a prisoner of war for a year (there being no Geneva Convention, things were rough). After his release, he had a complete physical and mental breakdown, followed by a very gradual recovery. When he tried to piece together the shattered fragments of his life, he found they wouldn't go back the right way, but insisted on making a new pattern that frightened but also excited him. At its center was—well, Francis said God, but if God doesn't make sense for you, call it the Oneness of everything, benign and gracious and inexpressibly tender toward all that exists.

Francis felt the embrace of God and saw with a pang that he had been conniving in a tragic sham, one that God longed to undo. God's Son Jesus died for wanting to open people's eyes to their folly and convince them that happiness is in reaching out, not in shutting out. Elbowing others aside so I can grab more for myself may seem like a good idea, but it conflicts with the way we've been made and doing it is doing violence to my real self. We've all got one Father and everything is related, and so Francis with unassailable logic began to call everybody and everything "sister" and "brother." This wasn't just a romantic affectation. It was the manifesto of a campaign.

Francis spent his life trying to convince us that we're free only when we accept responsibility for everyone and for all creation. His most unforgettable lessons are the things he does:

He stands before the people of Assisi and strips off all his clothes, for by clothes people are divided and categorized—but this is not our truth.

He constantly gives away what has been given to him, because to keep something when someone else needs it more is stealing—and this is not our truth.

He refuses to be the owner of any house or place or thing, because what you own you must defend—and this cannot be our truth.

He embraces and kisses the leper thrust out by town and family, and in so doing is conscious that he is the one who is blessed—and this he knows to be our truth.

He makes friends with the fierce wolf of Gubbio and shows the people it is hunger that has made him a killer—and they come to see that this is our truth.

He walks unarmed through the din of battle to speak of love and peace to the sultan of Egypt and is heard with reverence—for this is assuredly our truth.

He speaks to the birds of the air and invites them to give thanks to the One

who made them and all that lives—
and they too seem to know that this
is our truth.

He sings the praises of God Most High,
whose love and care is seen in sun and
moon, in earth and air and water, in
people who tenderly care for one another,
and even in our sister death—and here is
the heart of our truth.

Francis tries everything he can think of to
jolt us into seeing and feeling the truth that
is so clear to him. We need that jolt, badly.
We need to see with new eyes the blasphemy
of being comfortable while God's children
suffer and starve to death, of daring to pray
to God when we are indifferent to the fate
of the sisters and the brothers God has
asked us to cherish. "Receivers of stolen
goods" is Francis' phrase for us when we
cocoon ourselves in comfort when millions
have nothing.

The book you are holding in your hands
is dangerous and should probably carry a
government health warning. Gerry Straub is
a modern-day Francis, jolting us into the
truth by the power of images. You may be
glad or sorry you opened this book, but you
can't set it down and remain as you were
before you picked it up: Whatever you do

now is a decision. There's no neutral option.
You will either do something—or you reject
your truth, our truth, the truth at the heart
of everything.

When Francis looked back, at the end
of a fairly short life, on the decision he had
made twenty years before, he tells how it
affected him. "What I used to find so
disgusting," he says, "was changed into my
greatest satisfaction and joy." When I stop
being a "thief" and begin to go straight, the
same will happen to me. Try it and see.

PART ONE

A Photographic Meditation

Manila, the Philippines

Wang'uru, Kenya

Kingston, Jamaica

Manila, the Philippines

Nairobi, Kenya

Kingston, Jamaica

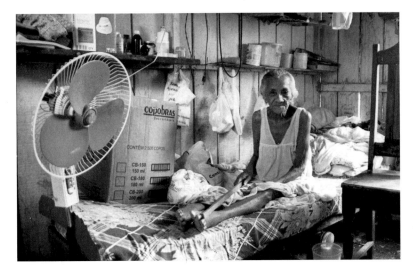

Manaus, Brazil

Kingston, Jamaica

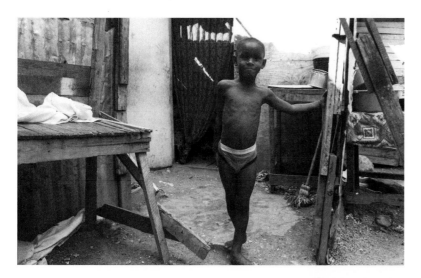

Kingston, Jamaica

Kingston, Jamaica

Chennai, India

Nairobi, Kenya

Nairobi, Kenya

Kingston, Jamaica

Chennai, India

Juarez, Mexico

Kingston, Jamaica

Nairobi, Kenya

Manaus, Brazil

Calcutta, India

Manaus, Brazil

Manila, the Philippines

Manila, the Philippines

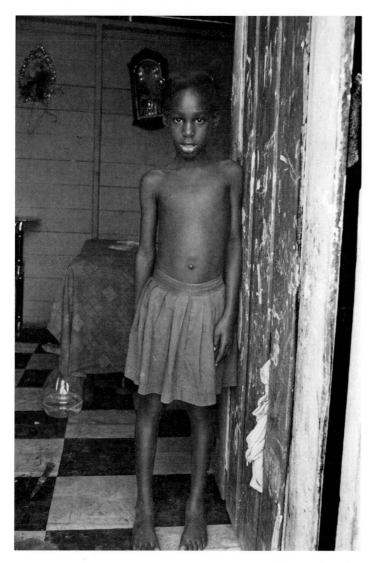

Kingston, Jamaica

Kingston, Jamaica

Kingston, Jamaica

15

Nairobi, Kenya

Nairobi, Kenya

Manaus, Brazil

Rangjuli, India

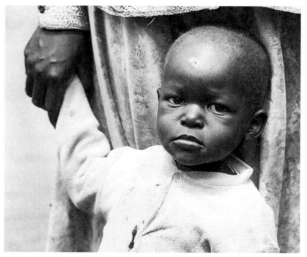

Nairobi, Kenya

Kingston, Jamaica

Wang'uru, Kenya

Bangalore, India

Manila, the Philippines

Wang'uru, Kenya

Calcutta, India

San Francisco, California

Manaus, Brazil

Nairobi, Kenya

Nairobi, Kenya

Nairobi, Kenya

Wang'uru, Kenya

Nairobi, Kenya

Chennai, India

Kingston, Jamaica

Nairobi, Kenya

Manaus, Brazil

Nairobi, Kenya

Manila, the Philippines

Kingston, Jamaica

St. Catherine, Jamaica

Nairobi, Kenya

Nairobi, Kenya

MURRAY BODO, O.F.M.

Author of *Francis: The Journey and the Dream, The Way of St. Francis, Legends of St. Francis* and *Clare: A Light in the Garden*

"Lord, when was it that we saw you hungry and gave you food, or thirsty and gave you something to drink? And when was it that we saw you a stranger and welcomed you, or naked and gave you clothing? And when was it that we saw you sick or in prison and visited you?" And the king will answer them, "Truly I tell you, just as you did it to one of the least of these who are members of my family, you did it to me." —MATTHEW 25:37–40

WE LOOK AT THESE PHOTOGRAPHS. They are relentlessly what we don't want to see. And yet we're drawn into them. We remember something we've forgotten, something perhaps we didn't know we knew. It has something to do with questions like, Who is my brother and sister? Why is the Christian God born of poor parents in a stable at Bethlehem? Why did Jesus say, "Blessed are the poor in spirit; the kingdom of God is theirs"? We wonder, Does the kingdom of heaven happen therefore where there is poverty of spirit? And are the real poor always poor in spirit, or mostly angry, bitter victims of those who are not poor? What is poverty? Shouldn't we be spending our time eradicating poverty rather than visiting the poor? Or do the poor teach us something only they know? Is theirs the secret of life's meaning, or is that just a romanticizing of failure—theirs and ours?

Already the questions overwhelm us. They paralyze our ability to respond with compassion to the photos. And all the while we have reduced the faces in these pictures to a generality: the poor. They do have names, these homeless ones, these poor people we pass by hoping they will not approach us, panhandle us, tell us some well-rehearsed hard-luck story. They are just blurred faces, shadow figures in the alleys and dark corners of deteriorating neighborhoods. They are not just "them," the homeless, the unlocated poor. They do have names, and that is where we visit them, in their names that have become their homes. "When I was a stranger, you took me into your home," Jesus says. The stranger has no name; the guest does. To welcome the stranger as a guest is to learn his or her name and to offer our name in return. And that can only be done person to person, which is where love begins.

Love is learning the names of people and things, and not waiting until all our questions are answered before we begin. These photos give us faces. Only the charity of visiting people like those whose images beckon us here will reveal their names. Then, in the exchange of names, much of what we need to know about ourselves and the other will be revealed to us.

What we learn, first of all, is that we are all ultimately homeless on this earth, our hearts never at rest until they rest in God, as Saint Augustine said so pointedly centuries ago. We learn, too, what Saint Francis of Assisi saw with visionary eyes, namely, that what we relegate to the periphery of society, what we marginalize and exclude, is also what we fear we really are or could become. And when we embrace that fear in flesh-and-blood human beings, we find our own goodness and beauty—and theirs.

These photos see the beauty and goodness of the individual face; their challenge is the challenge of love: Will black and white images on a page lead us to find the names they live in, the real people they represent, and in doing so, find our names, as well? If so, then ours will be the experience of Saint Francis, who wrote in his last Testament, "For I, being in sin, thought it bitter to look at lepers, and the Lord himself led me among them, and I worked mercy with them. And when I left their company, I realized that what had seemed bitter to me, had been turned into sweetness of soul and body."

This book is just such an invitation to sweetness. As images of the poor have led Gerard Straub to discover their names in all the parts of the world, so now the faces he has returned with lead us in turn to learn the names of the faces in our town, our own neighborhood. For charity, as we know, begins at home. Like Saint Francis, sweetness of soul and body awaits us just outside the comfortable world we have made for ourselves.

PART TWO

A Meditation in Images and Words

Detroit, Michigan

Saint Francis, Assisi, Italy

SAINT FRANCIS OF ASSISI's love of God led him to a deep appreciation of poverty and a firm commitment to help those in need. The words and images in this book are meant to try to capture the essence of the saint's courtship with Lady Poverty and help us to embrace the poor and our own poverty.

Saint Francis of Assisi encountered God in the dwelling places of the lepers. The lepers helped the saint understand and heal himself. Today, we encounter lepers all the time. They are the homeless sleeping on park benches or in crime-ridden shelters. They are the deinstitutionalized mental patients begging on our corners. They are the jobless offering to wash our car windows. They are the poor children dying from preventable diseases. They are the refugees flooding across borders with nothing but the clothes on their backs and hope in their hearts. They are the drug addicts and alcoholics sleeping in subways and vacant buildings. They are the truly destitute eating in soup kitchens where day-old bread and doughnuts are served. They are the AIDS victims dying alone in hospices. Today's lepers are the two-thirds of humanity who live in crippling poverty. Enter their dwelling places and share their misery, and encounter the love and mercy of God.

Chennai, India

Not until the creation and maintenance of decent conditions of life for all people are recognized and accepted as a common obligation of all people and all countries— not until then shall we, with a certain degree of justification, be able to speak of mankind as civilized.

—ALBERT EINSTEIN, *Great Words of Our Time*

Compassion is far removed from pity and sympathy. Compassion grows out of an awareness of our common humanity.

Nairobi, Kenya

Nairobi, Kenya

Half of humanity must survive on the equivalent of two dollars a day, or less. Half of that half lives on less than one dollar a day.

Rome, Italy

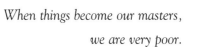

When things become our masters,
we are very poor.

—MOTHER TERESA, quoted in *Everything Starts with Prayer: Mother Teresa's Meditations on Spiritual Life for People of All Faiths*

Toronto, Canada

We do not fully welcome Christ if we are not ready to welcome the poor person with whom He has identified Himself.

—RANIERO CANTALAMESSA, O.F.M. CAP., *Poverty*

Rome, Italy

We need each other. None of us is truly rich, and sooner or later each of us suffers from ignoring the other. It is our mutual privilege to give to one another.

—RUTH BURROWS, *Living Love*

Nearly 800 million people do not have access to adequate food and nutrition. Of those, 200 million are children.

Bangalore, India

Kingston, Jamaica

Malnutrition causes the deaths of over 6 million children under the age of 5 every year. Imagine, if you can . . . in developing countries, 1 child in 10 never celebrates a fifth birthday because hunger robbed the child of life.

In the United States, 1 in 10 households
live with hunger. In those homes,
36 million people, including 12 million
children, are forced to skip meals
or eat less to make ends meet.

Philadelphia, Pennsylvania

Philadelphia, Pennsylvania

The widespread existence of hunger is a massive violation of human rights bordering on epidemic proportions.

Am I a part of a system of oppression of the poor? Unless I stand with the poor, the answer is "yes."

Juarez, Mexico

37

Chennai, India

To learn the causes of poverty, we must spend time with the poor. If we share in their struggles, we can share in their liberation.

Philadelphia, Pennsylvania

The essence of Jesus' message is: Make every stranger, no matter how poor or dirty, no matter how weak or unlovable, your neighbor. Tough message.

Rome, Italy

To turn your back on the poor is to turn your back on Jesus.

Chennai, India

The poor, the weak and the hurting are God made visible.

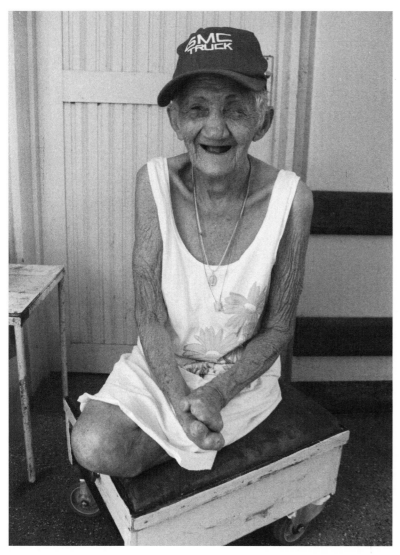

Manaus, Brazil

This old woman suffers from leprosy. Her life is overwhelmingly difficult and lonely. Yet, I could see the joy on her face when I stopped to spend some time with her. Moments before taking this photograph, I asked her how she was doing. Her answer stunned me. "Very, very good—praise be to God."

The richest 20 percent of the world's population consumes 85 percent of all goods and services. The poorest 20 percent of the world's population consumes 1 percent of all goods and services.

Kingston, Jamaica

Nairobi, Kenya

Wise consumption is much more complicated than wise production. What five people will produce, one person can very easily consume, and the question for each individual and for every nation is not how are we to produce, but how our products are to be consumed.

—JOHN RUSKIN,
from *A Calendar of Wisdom* by Leo Tolstoy

The more goods I keep for my own enjoyment,
the less there are for others. My pleasures
and comforts are, in a certain sense,
taken from someone else.

—THOMAS MERTON, *No Man Is an Island*

Nairobi, Kenya

Chennai, India

Consuming more than you need is stealing from those in need.

As long as we enjoy comfort and require security, it will be impossible to have true compassion for the poor and the weak.

Bangalore, India

Manila, the Philippines

Once we begin not to worry about what kind of house we are living in, what kind of clothes we are wearing, we have time, which is priceless, to remember that we are our brother's keeper, and that we must not only care for his needs as far as we are immediately able, but try to build a better world

—DOROTHY DAY, from an unpublished manuscript quoted in *Breaking Bread: The Catholic Worker and the Origin of Catholic Radicalism in America* by Mel Pieh

Nairobi, Kenya

The poor taught me to see the barrenness of affluence and the emptiness of consumerism.

Manila, the Philippines

This little girl is no different than I am.
We are both weak and vulnerable...
just in different ways.

Relinquishing the possessions of the ego we all amass inside ourselves is the most demanding form of poverty.

Nairobi, Kenya

Manaus, Brazil

Every act of mercy and kindness brings us closer to the reality of God.

Dependence on God may be what is lacking in
a society where consumerism and accumulation
have become the root diseases of a world
in which everything is not enough
and nothing satisfies.

—JOAN CHITTISTER,
The Rule of Benedict: Insights for the Ages

Juarez, Mexico

53

Rome, Italy

What does a rejected person want? It is a real look of understanding, a look of compassion and even of wonderment—to be treated as a unique person.

—JEAN VANIER, *Followers of Jesus*

The greatest violation of poverty is to hold onto the good God gives—goodness must flow.

Guwahati, India

Toronto, Canada

The constant barrage of belittlement hurled their way, coupled with the isolation they endure, make life on the streets for the homeless person a bigger psychological than physical challenge.

Salinas, California

Jesus invited the poor and the outcasts to sit at his banquet table. Who are our dinner guests?

Manila, the Philippines

Giving food to the poor is easy. Eating with the poor is much harder...and much more rewarding. Jesus ate with the poor, and he asks us to do the same. Communion with the poor is an enriching source of healing.

In the Sermon on the Mount, Jesus said the hungry will be satisfied. It can happen—but only when we stand in solidarity with the poor and accompany them on their journey.
As we walk together, common concern will overcome the destructive tendencies of individualism and greed.

Philadelphia, Pennsylvania

Kingston, Jamaica

The gospel compels us to unite with the poor in their struggle against poverty. We are all outraged when human rights are violated by terrorism, repression and murder. But where is the outrage when human rights are violated by the existence of dire conditions of extreme poverty and unjust economic structures that give rise to vast inequalities?

Solidarity with the poor is a
protest against poverty.

Nairobi, Kenya

Kingston, Jamaica

Service to the poor is not optional—it is a requirement for the follower of Jesus.

Manila, the Philippines

The poor see reality with a clarity of vision that is rarely reached by the comfortable. Walking among the impoverished improves our vision. We are able to see injustice and feel pain. We see how dehumanizing dire poverty is, and we want to join in their struggle for liberation from the chains that bind them.

Juarez, Mexico

Today's global economy fosters soulless consumerism and a mindless worship of technology, while trampling the rights of workers and the poor.

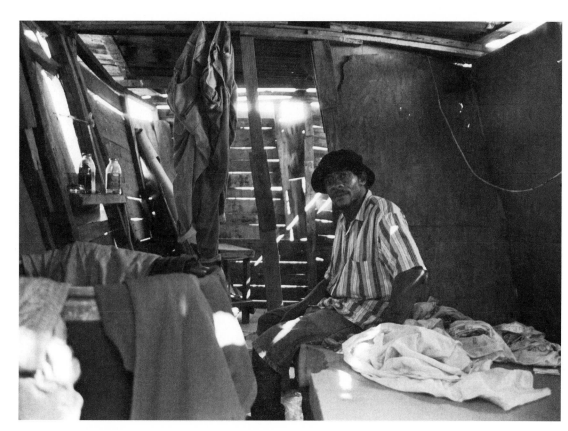

Exposure to those saddled with dire poverty
uncovers our clinging selfishness.

Kingston, Jamaica

Chennai, India

We have become so isolated from the poor and the suffering that we have lost the chance to find true fulfillment by giving of ourselves.

Film and television star Dick van Dyke spends Thanksgiving Day at a skid-row soup kitchen.

Los Angeles, California

Juarez, Mexico

The Gospels make it abundantly clear that God is on the side
of the poor, the broken in body and spirit and the outcasts
of society, the lepers, the prostitutes, the orphans...
and today we must add the addicted.

Did you bring good news to the poor today?

Manila, the Philippines

Juarez, Mexico

A concern for where the poor are to sleep will make us realize that it is in fact not possible to separate love of God and love of neighbor; that is, that we must live both aspects as intertwined with each other. When we experience things at their root, we are helped in seeing the unity of our life is not created by a fine, balanced formulation of ideas, but by taking the path of practicing love of God and love of neighbor in one and the same act. This alone will lead us to life. The journey is a costly one but also full of hope, because on it we gradually become compassionate as the God in whom we believe is compassionate.

—GUSTAVO GUTIERREZ,
  Gustavo Gutierrez: Essential Writings

More than a third of humanity
lacks sanitary toilets.

Juarez, Mexico

Rangjuli, India

Every minute of every day 10 children under the age of 5 die of hunger or diseases related to hunger.

The true moral fiber of any society or community or family is revealed by how it treats its weakest member.

Chennai, India

Wang'uru, Kenya

Spend five minutes a day thinking about how you can prudently do something for the most vulnerable members of your neighborhood.

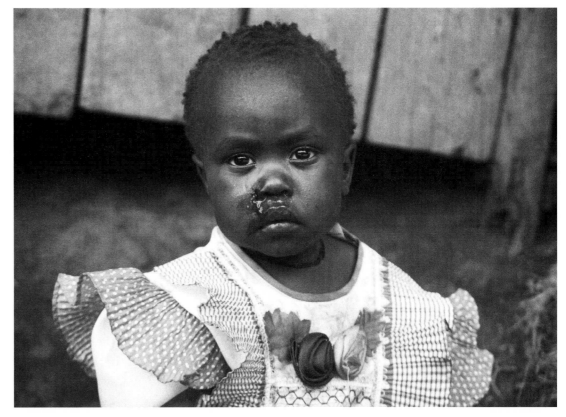

Nairobi, Kenya

The basic health needs of the world's poorest people could be provided for less money than Americans and Europeans spend each year on pet food.

Bangalore, India

And what you hate, do not do to anyone….Give some of your food to the hungry, and some of your clothing to the naked.

—TOBIT 4:15–16

Jesus shows us that mercy is more than compassion or justice. Mercy requires us to become one with the poor and hurting, to live their misery as though it were our own. Jesus took his place with the condemned, an innocent deliberately allowing himself to be arrested. God's love gives everything, always.

Kingston, Jamaica

Manaus, Brazil

We do not detach ourselves from things in order to attach ourselves to God, but rather we become detached from ourselves in order to see and use all things in and for God.

—THOMAS MERTON, *New Seeds of Contemplation*

Those who do not see the meaning of their life in temporary things, in their names and bodies, those people know the truth of life.

—THE DHAMMAPADA

Kingston, Jamaica

79

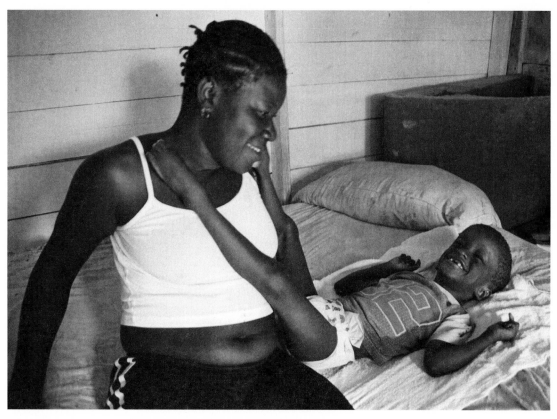

Kingston, Jamaica

All suffering comes from cherishing ourselves.
All happiness comes from cherishing others.

—TIBETAN SAYING

We can truly love only when our hearts are free of the self-centered desires of pride, ambition and lust.

Bangalore, India

Kingston, Jamaica

Acts of charity are the wings of love.

God's love excludes no one.

Chennai, India

All life is a cry to God.

Makati City, the Philippines

Every person is wounded by one's family or
by society. Each of us is in need of healing.
Each person has an infinite capacity for growth
and that growth will resume its rightful course
as soon as it is given an opportunity and the
adequate environment is created. Every child is
completely dependent; left to oneself, he or she
is psychologically incapable of coping with life.
Children need to be accepted and protected by
someone else. The child must feel that someone
is so concerned with her that she has been
drawn into the safety of the orbit of their life.
Only then is the vacuum of the child's
dependency filled, only then is he in a
condition in which natural growth and
development can take place.

—EDWARD FARRELL, *Free to Be Nothing*

Manila, the Philippines

Nairobi, Kenya

Life's most urgent question is,
what are we doing for others?

—MARTIN LUTHER KING, JR.

Nairobi, Kenya

There is a splendor in poor things,
the splendor of what is real.

—ERNESTO CARDENAL, *Abide in Love*

Rome, Italy

God loves us because we are weak and powerless, not in spite of those qualities. We need to accept that we are all poor and needy, and that only God can lift us up.

At Christmas, we send old clothes and checks to local churches but still feel at odds with the poor. Afraid of placing ourselves at economic risk we offer what is spare and worn and given at a distance. The problem, however, is not with what we give away or how, but with what we keep for ourselves.

—ALICE CALLAGHAN, director of Las Familias del Puebla in Los Angeles, from the *Los Angeles Times*, December 24, 1999

Los Angeles, California

Manila, the Philippines

Manila, the Philippines

While the prosperous around the world
are sipping bottled spring water, nearly
2 million people living in poverty are forced
to drink and bathe in water contaminated
with deadly parasites and pathogens.

Grace is God's way of talking to us. We can
best experience grace and therefore hear
God more clearly when we stop living for
ourselves and instead give ourselves in
loving service to others.

All we can give God is our needs.

If we develop compassion, other spiritual experiences will naturally rise within us. Compassion is the root of all virtues. It can free us from grasping at self.

—TULKU THONDUP RINPOCHE,
The Healing Power of Mind: Simple Meditation Exercises for Health, Well-Being and Enlightenment

Manila, the Philippines

Salinas, California

The greedy tendencies of the ego and its insatiable hunger for possessions rob us of our wholeness. We become whole again when the self learns how to be empty, willing to lose itself in order to enter into a deep and rich communion with others.

The primary aspiration of all history is a genuine community of human beings.

—MARTIN BUBER

Makati City, the Philippines

Nairobi, Kenya

Community is the womb of love.
In community, love is planted,
nurtured and birthed.

Kingston, Jamaica

We must all work to create a society that is founded on welcome and respect, embracing the most vulnerable among us.

95

Manila, the Philippines

God did not create poverty. People created poverty. And we can also end it.

The right to food is a basic human right.

Calcutta, India

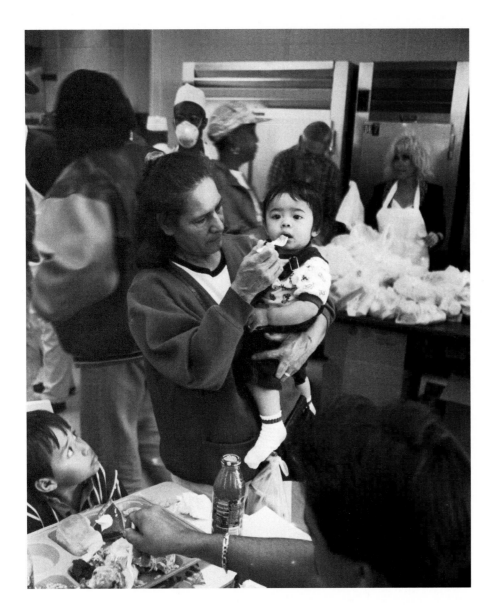

Hunger has no borders; nor does it discriminate.

Los Angeles, California

Lack of food is not the reason for hunger.
Hunger exists because the poor lack
the money to buy food.

Calcutta, India

Calcutta, India

The poor in developing countries spend half of their income on food.

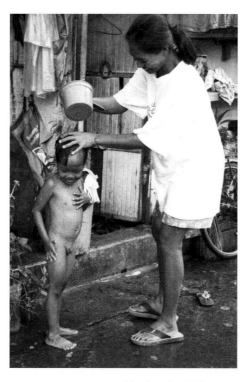

Manila, the Philippines

A mother bathing her naked child on the street is a common sight in Manila.

Manila, the Philippines

101

Manila, the Philippines

[E]very man has the right to possess a sufficient amount of the earth's goods for himself and his family.

—Pastoral Constitution on the Church in the Modern World [*Gaudium et spes*]

WHEN I FIRST CAME TO JAMAICA twenty-five years ago, I was young, enthusiastic and full of pride. I thought I could set the world on fire, could save the poor. Didn't happen. Instead, the poor set my heart on fire. Through their faith, the poor liberated me.

The poor taught me what it truly means to depend on God for everything and not on my own strengths. In the process of serving them—the abandoned, the sick, those with leprosy and the dying—I was the one who was converted and empowered to see Christ through the struggles, the pain and suffering the poor experience on a daily basis.

There is nothing romantic about working with the poor. It is tough, frustrating, dirty work that can even be dangerous at times. But, working with the poor is also a source of true joy and transforming grace. The poor taught me how to follow Christ—how to love the way he would, how to be more accepting, forgiving and merciful. The poor have given me more than I have given them...they gave me the chance to slowly become more like Christ, even though I have a long way to go and often fail to live up to his demanding standards.

Don't shut out the poor. Open the door of your heart to them and they will open your heart to the true meaning of love: to give your self completely.

Monsignor Richard Albert
Stella Maris Church
Kingston, Jamaica

Kingston, Jamaica

Monsignor Richard Albert talking with a man who lives in the slums on the edge of the Riverton garbage dump.

Kingston, Jamaica

Every day, hundreds of people rummage through the garbage dump in the Riverton section of Kingston searching for anything they can salvage and sell.

Riverton garbage dump, Kingston, Jamaica

Philadelphia, Pennsylvania

Every night more than 700,000 Americans are without shelter.

Nowhere in the United States is the minimum wage of one person sufficient to allow for the rental of a two-bedroom apartment at the fair market rent. Moreover, nearly 5 million families pay half their income for rent.

Philadelphia, Pennsylvania

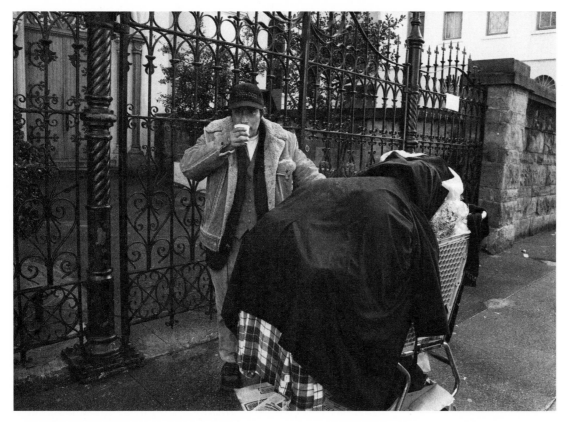

San Francisco, California

Every night, more than 7,000 homeless people wander the streets of San Francisco. Shelters can provide a bed for only 1,500 of them.

To whitewash injustice is in itself an injustice.

Manila, the Philippines

Philadelphia, Pennsylvania

In our encounters with the poor, we must move from pity to love, from charity to justice.

The seduction of possessions blinds us to the needs of the poor.

Kingston, Jamaica

When profit is the aim and law of life, then humanity suffers a great loss.

112

Albuquerque, New Mexico

As we have learned from ecology, all things are interconnected, and in today's global economy, the same is true of our consumer choices. They have wide-ranging, often global implications. To remind ourselves of these implications, read the following slowly. In the last two hundred years the United States has lost: 50% of its wetlands 90% of its Northwestern old growth forests, and 99% of its tall grass prairie. Average time spent shopping per week: 6 hours; average time spent playing with children per week: 40 minutes. The amount of energy used by one American is equivalent to that used by 3 Japanese, 14 Chinese, or 168 Bangladeshi people.

—MICHAEL SCHUT, *ed., Simpler Living,*
Compassionate Life: A Christian Perspective

St. Catherine, Jamaica

Our wealth lies in God's love for us; our poverty lies in our lack of love for God.

114

Jesus embraced simplicity, poverty and humility. What do we embrace?

Kingston, Jamaica

Nairobi, Kenya

The road to God is straight and narrow: the road is poverty. We must be willing to go to God with empty hands, trusting God for everything.

The world demands more and more from us.
God asks only for empty hands.

Nairobi, Kenya

Kingston, Jamaica

We find it more comfortable to put limits on God, and in doing so we create a spiritual poverty within us.

We must become the poor Christ...offered up and given away.

El Paso, Texas

Kingston, Jamaica

Only when I am vulnerable is it possible for me to be broken and restored to the image of God.

Breaking the bondage of egoism is the toughest task in life. Liberation is difficult and painful.

Nairobi, Kenya

Nairobi, Kenya

In the state of emptiness, you are better able to encounter the fullness of God.

To run from the experience of poverty is to run from God.

Nairobi, Kenya

Nairobi, Kenya

To become poor in spirit is to know the richness of God.

Rangjuli, India

Poverty of spirit frees us from the tyranny of wealth.

Nairobi, Kenya

Love is the only antidote to selfishness.

Thoughtfulness is the beginning of great sanctity.

—MOTHER TERESA, quoted in *Works of Love Are Works of Peace: Mother Teresa of Calcutta and the Missionaries of Charity* by Michael Collopy

Detroit, Michigan

127

Philadelphia, Pennsylvania

Acts of love give flesh to faith and hope.

Poverty helps me see beauty
in an earthenware pot.

Chennai, India

Rangjuli, India

Simplicity immunizes you against the plague of consumerism.

Justice should compel us to meet
the needs of the poor.

Kingston, Jamaica

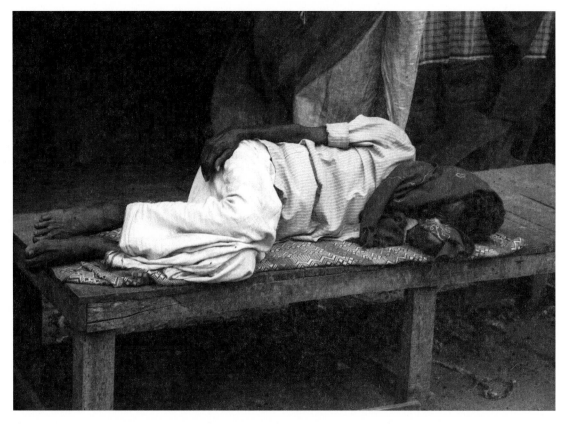

Chennai, India

If you want to show gratitude to God, be generous to others.

The virtue of poverty is that it leads one to recognize that God alone can provide us with what we truly need.

Chennai, India

Kingston, Jamaica

Giving a few dollars to the poor is not the same as being one with the poor, which is what Christ requires.

134

The deceitfulness of riches is the confusion between what we have and what we are.

—ERNESTO CARDENAL,
Abide in Love

Rangjuli, India

135

Jemez Pueblo, New Mexico

To share is to break the bread of our lives...to give our hearts, our hopes, our dreams, our thoughts, our time.

The best way to love God is to relieve the pain and suffering of others.

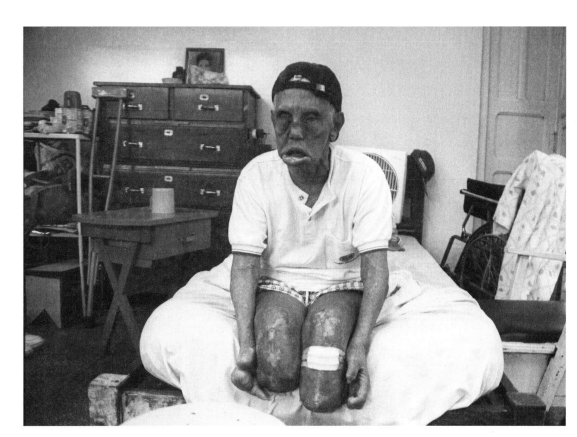

Manaus, Brazil

Chennai, India

My awareness of God's mysterious presence within me makes me more aware of the same presence within others.

Lord, give bread to the hungry and hunger for You to those who have bread.

—CATHERINE DOHERTY

San Francisco, California

139

Could you look a hungry, crying child in the eye and say, "The problem of hunger is beyond our means to solve; I am sorry, but there is nothing I can do"?

Manila, the Philippines

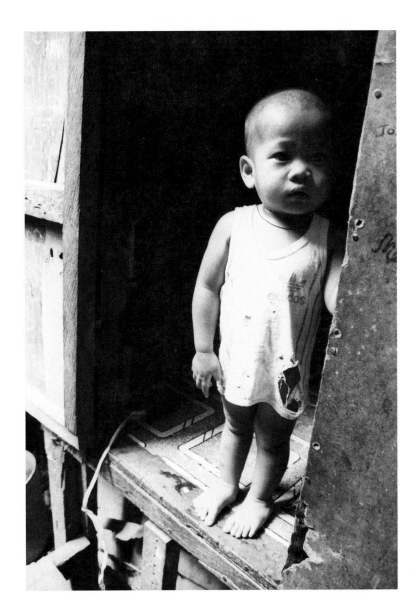

The innocence of childhood is quickly
stolen from the children of poverty.

Manila, the Philippines

141

Manila, the Philippines

They see and feel the harsh reality of life at a very early age.

Nairobi, Kenya

Children should not have to live with fear and rejection.

Juarez, Mexico

In Juarez, Mexico, I met a 14-year-old boy who dropped out of school because he worked 16 hours a day at two menial jobs to help his handicapped mother and seriously ill father feed his two little brothers. The boy had no time for dreams of his own future. He was too busy fighting for survival today.

A little girl in Manila told a Franciscan priest she did not want to tell her mother she was sick, because she knew the mother did not have the money for medicine. The priest understood, because he has met many mothers who stopped taking their own medicine in order to buy medicine for their children. And then there is the real and constant threat of the pain of hunger...for parents and children.

Manila, the Philippines

145

Nairobi, Kenya

As you look at these children, these children of God, think how you, in your own special way, can touch the life of some poor child in your neighborhood.

Detroit, Michigan

Many poor parents, despite holding down one or more jobs, cannot afford to feed their children adequately and are forced to rely on soup kitchens for survival. And without volunteer help, soup kitchens could not survive. It is a great joy to serve a child a hot meal.

This young boy just finished eating lunch at a soup kitchen run by Capuchin Franciscans. Behind him is a photo of people eating in the same soup kitchen during the 1920's.

Detroit, Michigan

Detroit, Michigan

Before I began spending time at soup kitchens, I thought only the elderly and homeless ate at them, and I would never have guessed that so many children depend on them for their main meal of the day.

Detroit, Michigan

A friar talks to a family in a soup kitchen.

Home.

Ensenada, Mexico

School.

Nairobi, Kenya

San Quintin, Mexico

And this is home for two small children and their handicapped mother.

They live in a migrant farm-worker camp.

San Quintin, Mexico

Los Angeles, California

The homeless: we brush them from our minds because their misery might disturb our otherwise beautiful day.

Jesus embraced, touched and loved the poor, the outcasts and the rejected. He called them "blessed." For Jesus, the poor and lowly are sacraments because they offer a direct way to encounter God.

Philadelphia, Pennsylvania

Manila, the Philippines

The message of love of the crucified and transfigured Christ compels us to judge no one, to exclude no one; moreover, it requires us to help others to carry their cross, fully sharing in their pain and suffering.

This young woman, who has no arms or legs, guides a blind boy through the barrio.

156

For the Christian there is no stranger. Whoever is near us and needing us must be "our neighbor"; it does not matter whether he is related to us or not, whether we like him or not, whether he is morally worthy of our help or not. The love of Christ knows no limits. It never ends; it does not shrink from ugliness and filth. He came for sinners, not for the just. And if the love of Christ is in us we shall do as He did and seek the lost sheep.

—EDITH STEIN (Saint Teresa Benedicta of the Cross), "The Mystery of Christmas," quoted in *Selected Writings of Edith Stein*, translated and edited by Hilda C. Graef

Manila, the Philippines

We can discover our true selves only through the sincere gift of ourselves.

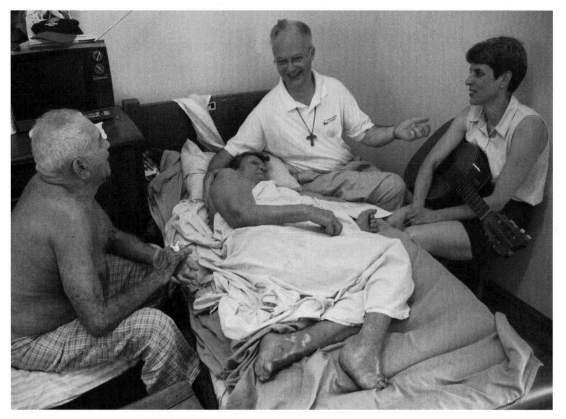

Manaus, Brazil

The deepest wisdom man can attain is to know that his destiny is to aid and serve.

—Abraham Joshua Heschel, *Man Is Not Alone*

Jim Flickinger, a Secular Franciscan, is a lawyer from Grand Rapids, Michigan, who brings aid to lepers in the Amazon region of Brazil through his charitable organization, Amazon Relief.

158

We are all created by the Creator, and so
we are all in relationship with one another.
We are all brothers and sisters, and to set
yourself up as higher or better than others is
a subtle form of blasphemy. We are all
connected. If one among us is diminished,
we are all diminished. We are one with all
of creation and the Creator. We must seek
harmony in diversity as we rejoice in our
humanness. The Incarnation compels us to
step to the back of the bus and sit with the
poor, to learn to see life from their point of
view so as to better share in their struggle
for access to God's gifts of freedom, oneness
and love that have been denied to
them by virtue of our selfishness.

Manila, the Philippines

Rangjuli, India

The Incarnation of Jesus Christ epitomizes God's passion for the poor and the disinherited.

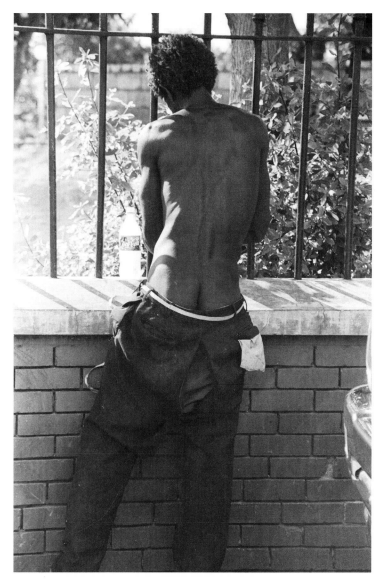

If we believe in the Incarnation of the Son of God, there should be no one on earth in whom we are not prepared to see, in mystery, the presence of Christ.

—THOMAS MERTON

Kingston, Jamaica

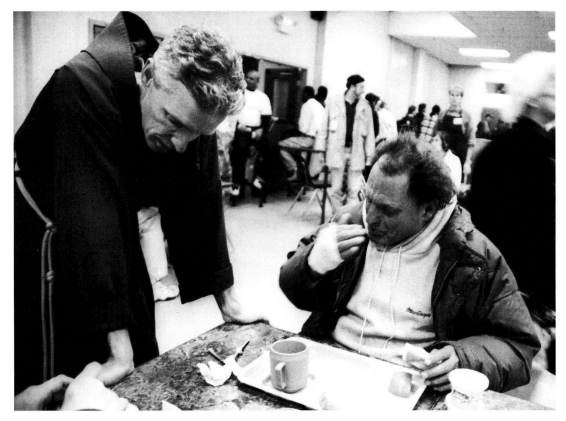

San Francisco, California

The mystery of the poor is this: That they are Jesus, and what you do for them you do for him.

—DOROTHY DAY, "The Mystery of the Poor," *The Catholic Worker,* April 1964

162

Chennai, India

But I, being poor, have only my dreams…Tread softly because you tread on my dreams.

—W. B. YEATS, "Aedh Wishes for the Cloths of Heaven," *The Wind Among the Reeds*

Manila, the Philippines

Although God's love embraces all people, God has clearly demonstrated deep concern for the poor and the needy, the helpless and the oppressed. God demands that we side with the poor, the powerless and victims of injustice. To walk with the poor is to be in harmony with the will of God.

Both the New and the Old Testaments reveal God's preferential love for those the world ignores and rejects.

Kingston, Jamaica

Nairobi, Kenya

Oh God, in your merciful goodness, forgive us the polarities and prejudices we have created and accepted within the human family which you created to live in peace, unity and harmony.

By loving the poor and insignificant first and foremost, God demonstrates the extent and fullness of divine love for all of creation.

Manila, the Philippines

167

Jemez Pueblo, New Mexico

Poverty touches Mother Earth also—when we take without regard to the consequences of our actions. To pollute our rivers, to strip our mountains of their trees, to fill the air with deadly toxins, is to impoverish future generations. Love and justice demand we treat earth as our sister, to nurture and protect her. Saint Francis of Assisi, who heard nature sing God's glory, reminds us that all creation is related and must live in communion. Every time an aspect of creation is disrespected, we lose another connection with the Creator.

Nairobi, Kenya

God hides in a piece of broken bread and in the broken life of a slum-dweller.

San Francisco, California

God wants us to see each other as tabernacles, as secret hiding places for the Divine. Pray for the grace to be able to see a homeless person as a tabernacle of God.

170

Action is as important as prayer; each of us must take responsibility for meeting the world's need, for we are the accomplices of evil if we do nothing to prevent it.

Bangalore, India

Manaus, Brazil

In condemning others, we avoid the more difficult task of knowing ourselves.

The lack of jobs and long-term
unemployment that plague the urban
slums increase the social isolation
of the inner-city poor.

Philadelphia, Pennsylvania

San Francisco, California

No one is self-sufficient. We need others and the Other.

Seeking the face of God in everything, everyone, everywhere, all the time and seeing His hand in every happening is contemplation. No contemplation is possible without asceticism and self abnegation.

—MOTHER TERESA, quoted in *Works of Love Are Works of Peace: Mother Teresa of Calcutta and the Missionaries of Charity* by Michael Collopy

Detroit, Michigan

PHOTO BY VINCENT REYES, O.F.M. CAP.

175

Detroit, Michigan

Christ has no body now on earth but yours; yours are the only hands with which he can do his work, yours are the only feet with which he can go about the world, yours are the only eyes through which his compassion can shine forth upon a troubled world. Christ has no body on earth but yours.

—SAINT TERESA OF AVILA, Traditional Prayer

176

Chennai, India

The spiritual life does not lift us out of the human condition, with its misery, problems, confrontations, pain and difficulties. Oh, but if only it did. The spiritual life plunges us more deeply into our humanity. It would be nice to sit in church all day, our hands clasped in prayer, drinking in the ecstasy of the Lord. But that is unrealistic; we must enter into the marketplace, walk the alleys of commerce. We must help each other out of the ditches we fall into. It is in the streets of life that we encounter God. Everything human is divine.

Philadelphia, Pennsylvania

Jesus instructed us never to think of ourselves as more important than others, never to put ourselves before anyone. His message is clear: Think little of yourself and be happy that others do not consider you very important. Moreover, Jesus asks us to stop struggling to control events for our own benefit and, instead, to try to be a servant to others.

178

Makati City, the Philippines

If Jesus was poor and humble, shouldn't we be also?

179

Manaus, Brazil

Hope is the fruit of charity.

San Francisco, California

Am I a sacrament of salvation for my neighbor?

Nairobi, Kenya

The hallmarks of authentic humanity are love and justice.

Justice requires that all people have a place to sleep, enough food to eat and work that makes them feel worthwhile.

Kingston, Jamaica

Kingston, Jamaica

Jesus came to liberate not oppress. Can I do anything other than what he did?

The life of Jesus illustrates that forgiveness and charity should have no limits.

Nairobi, Kenya

Kingston, Jamaica

Unconditional mercy requires total forgiveness with absolutely no conditions.

To place conditions on mercy and forgiveness is a form of violence.

186

What is God's will? Simple: love, mercy, justice, healing, peace and forgiveness.

Manila, the Philippines

Manila, the Philippines

We all crave to be on the receiving end of a gift of love, but our very craving masks a deeper, more profound human need: to give love.

At its root, there is only one reason for the existence of poverty: selfishness, which is a manifestation of a lack of authentic love.

Manila, the Philippines

Manila, the Philippines

Where do you draw the line on altruism?

190

*Every act of love is a work of peace
no matter how small.*

—MOTHER TERESA, quoted in *Works of Love Are
Works of Peace: Mother Teresa of Calcutta and
the Missionaries of Charity* by Michael Collopy

Nairobi, Kenya

The best way to eliminate hunger is to eliminate poverty.

Manila, the Philippines

Poverty isn't just a matter of not having sufficient income to live. Poverty isn't just living with hunger. The poor also experience a lack of a sense of well-being and peace of mind which so many of us take for granted. Poverty isn't about the lack of food, shelter and security; poverty is the rage you feel when you can't do anything about it. Poverty is the sense of hopelessness that kills the spirit.

Kingston, Jamaica

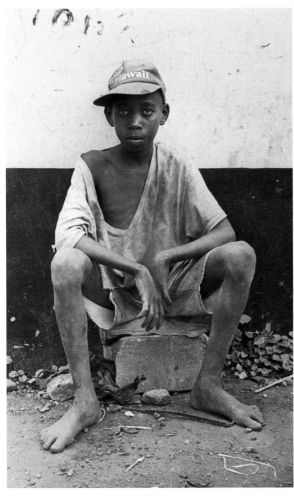

Wang'uru, Kenya

Who are the poorest of the poor? They are the 400 million or so people who spend 60 to 80 percent of their income on food but still lack sufficient calories to meet their metabolic needs. They are so undernourished that they are likely to suffer stunted growth, mental retardation or death.

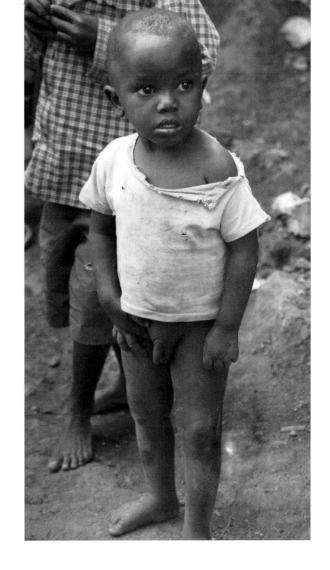

The combined gross domestic product of the 48 poorest nations, comprising nearly a quarter of the world's population, is less than the total wealth of the world's three richest people.

Nairobi, Kenya

Philadelphia, Pennsylvania

In the United States, over 30 million people live in households in which hunger is a constant threat.

As I traveled through dreadfully impoverished slums around the world, grace slowly taught me that those who "serve" the poor are the ones truly being served. I am the richer for having spent so much time among the poor. The Franciscan friars who housed and fed me as I worked and the wonderful people they selflessly serve helped me put my hand into the side of Christ.

Nairobi, Kenya

Nairobi, Kenya

Oh, how we long to find God in some moment of spiritual ecstasy, looking for the Divine in some spectacular or extraordinary event. Yet God comes to us, if we are to believe—fully believe—what Scripture says, in a humble disguise, in unexpected places. God comes to us poor, hungry, thirsty, diseased, imprisoned, alone and lonely. God comes to us in a homeless old woman forced to use a public street for a toilet. God comes to us in people, places and ways that make it difficult for us to see or receive God. We don't find God where we expect to or want to.

In metro Manila, just a short walk from opulent hotels featuring rooms for $300 a night, hundreds of people, using the only space available to them, are living in shacks alongside railroad tracks.

Makati City, the Philippines

Every week, a passing train hits a child or an old person who happens to stumble onto the tracks.

Makati City, the Philippines

Makati City, the Philippines

Try to imagine beginning your life beside a railroad track.

Manila, the Philippines

As I took these photographs of a young man bathing in the street, I could not help thinking how difficult that would be for me to do. I realized for the first time the richness of privacy. Then I thought about how truly pampered I am. To be able to spend as long as I wish in a nice hot shower is a luxury beyond the reach of millions of people around the world.

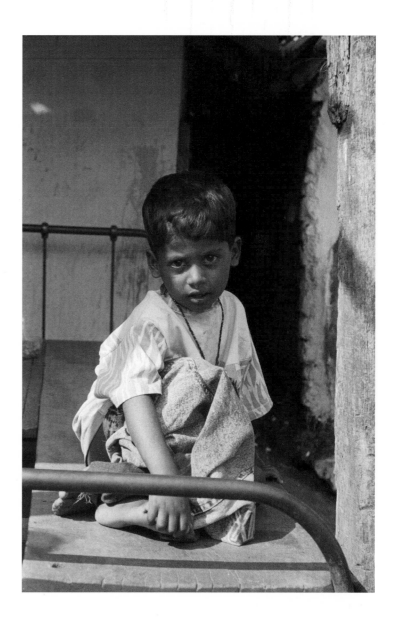

God grant me the grace truly to feel my intrinsic poverty.

Bangalore, India

St. Catherine, Jamaica

This is George. George is a leper. He lives at St. Monica's Home for the Abandoned and Elderly. The tune he is playing on the harmonica is "Amazing Grace." Amazing.

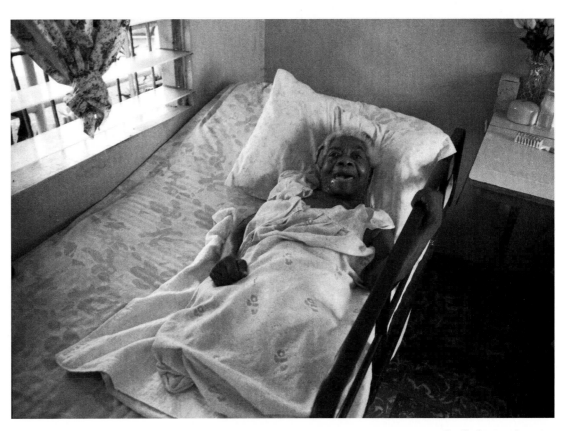

St. Catherine, Jamaica

This is Genevieve. She, too, lives at St. Monica's. She lost both legs but has not
lost her faith, which keeps her moving.

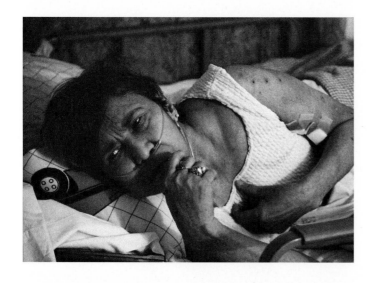

Albuquerque, New Mexico

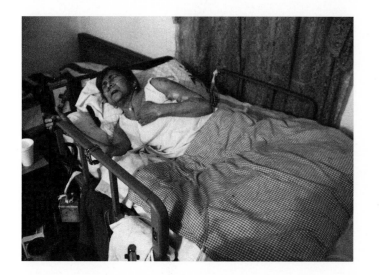

This is Melba Lopez. She is 69 years old. In 1945, when she was 14 years old, she fell from the roof of her home and was severely injured, losing both legs.

Melba's parents' severe poverty denied her access to adequate health care, and as a result she has been confined to her bed for the past 55 years. She is currently undergoing dialysis treatment three times a week.

Asked how she has endured her plight with such grace and humor, Melba said, "Every day I tell God the door is open and he is welcome to visit."

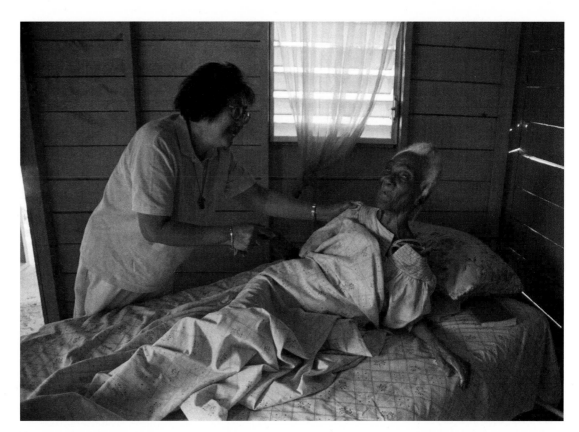

Kingston, Jamaica

A Franciscan sister visits a 103-year-old woman.

This is Gerda. She is 79 years old. She has intestinal cancer and is in the early stages of Alzheimer's disease. She has lived in this "hotel" room in San Francisco for 23 years. Gerda's room does not have a kitchen so she cooks her meager meals on a humble hot plate. She is one of the legions of elderly poor living a life of quiet destitution, tucked away and out of sight.

San Francisco, California

San Francisco, California

A Franciscan sister from St. Anthony's Foundation visits Gerda once a week, helping to break the isolation and loneliness of her sad life. Gerda said, "Sister brings me clothes and food, but most of all, she brings me love." Bringing love to the poor is part of living a gospel life.

Rangjuli, India

God is humble.

God lives in our poverty and weakness.

All good must be given back to God.

Chennai, India

Manila, the Philippines

Joy is never found in possessing.

Manaus, Brazil

If you greet sunrise with God in your heart and a prayer on your lips, there is a better chance that your day will reflect God's love, mercy and justice, and you will be better able to treat others the way God would.

213

Manila, the Philippines

The common good, which is the breath of freedom and the social bond between people, is being choked by the iron fist of individualism.

Kindness refreshes and restores
the tired and broken.

Nairobi, Kenya

Nairobi, Kenya

Faith and justice are soul mates whose hearts cry out for the poor.

Kingston, Jamaica

The commercial advertisements that fuel television deliver one common message: Do not be satisfied with what you have—only more "stuff" can make you happy.

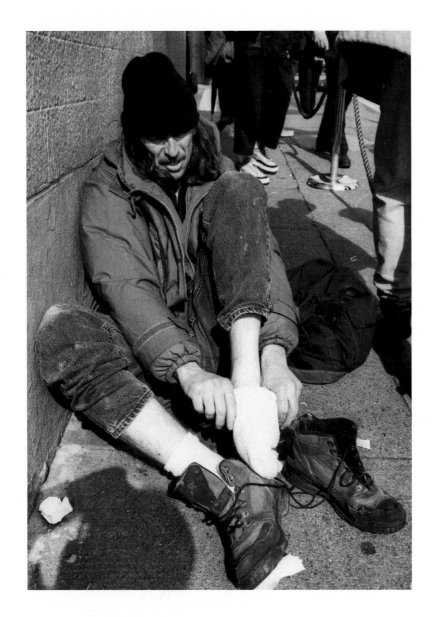

Feet. Most of us don't give them any thought. Not so for the homeless. Feet are always on their minds because they spend most of their time on them. The homeless stand for endless hours on lines for a sandwich at a soup kitchen, for medical assistance at clinic, for a bed at a shelter.

The old saying "walk a mile in my shoes" took on new meaning for me as I spent more time among the homeless...in my very expensive Ecco walking shoes from Denmark.

San Francisco, California

The largely undiscovered spiritual genius of the gospel is that Jesus refuses to take sides—in a human history that has always and everywhere taken sides. Jesus is on both sides of almost every war and every issue and every contentious group. Jesus is always on the side of the pain, using it to bring us to God. And the pain is on both sides: Jew and Arab, rich and poor, liberal and conservative, straight and gay, male and female, Christian and non-Christian. His gospel gives us precious little comfort if we want him to join our private club of anything, because the pain is everywhere, and the only experience that all human beings finally have in common. What genius that Jesus uses this universal suffering to bring us to God.

—RICHARD ROHR, O.F.M., Center for Action and Contemplation, Albuquerque, New Mexico

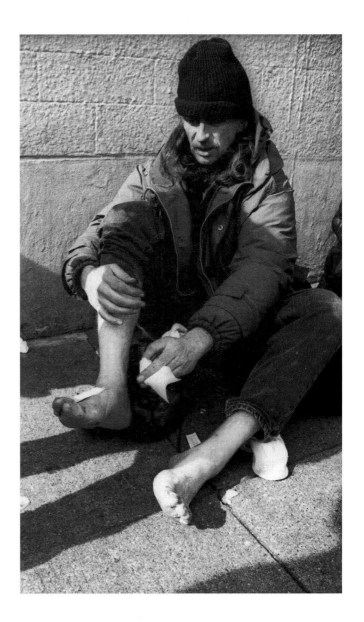

San Francisco, California

Payatas Garbage Dump, Manila, the Philippines

It was the saddest, most inhumane place I have ever seen. What I saw, smelt and felt was beyond imagination. The place is known as "Payatas." It is a giant garbage dump located on the outskirts of metropolitan Manila in the Philippines. Actually, Payatas is a mountain of garbage, stretching high into the sky. And the mountain is home to 75,000 people who live in and off the dump.

The people of Payatas earn their living scavenging through the waste of others. Entire families, including children as young as 4 years old, spend hours picking through garbage, searching for scraps of recyclable and reusable material they can salvage and sell for a few pennies. For most of them, this is the only life they know: a garbage dump. Scavenging is an arduous and hazardous life. Disease, such as tuberculosis, is rampant. Many of the children are disabled; most suffer from malnutrition. Their tiny bodies are infested with worms and covered with wounds received from sharp objects hidden in the garbage.

All day long, day in and day out, a relentless chain of garbage trucks slowly make their way up the muddy road to the peak. As the trucks dump the garbage, people are anxiously awaiting the chance to find something of worth, some discarded treasure in the garbage. The competition is fierce; fighting over the rubbish is common. Old women, young kids stoop over, feverishly using metal hooks to shift through the stinking, rotting debris. At the base of the mountain is a camp, a hellish hamlet of shacks where the garbage-pickers live. The place is a nightmare, a blight on society.

Payatas Garbage Dump, Manila, the Philippines

Payatas Garbage Dump, Manila, the Philippines

The Payatas scavengers are the lowliest of the urban poor. They truly are our *anawim*, the Old Testament term for the poorest of the poor, those completely ground down by want, without voice or rights in their surrounding community. Scripture makes it abundantly clear that to forget the *anawim*, is to forget God. Jesus made care for the *anawim* a litmus test for our love of God.

Payatas Garbage Dump, Manila, the Philippines

After spending so much time in the horrific slums of India and the Philippines, I thought nothing could shock me. But nothing could prepare a person for the horror of Payatas. After snapping a few rolls of film, I paused while reloading the camera. I turned to the Franciscan friar accompanying me and said, "I'll cry tonight." I kept taking pictures until I ran out of film and daylight. As I descended the mountain, my shoes and clothes muddied from the filth, I felt myself becoming sick from the smell. And from the reality that people are forced to live like this, like wild animals picking at the corpse of obsessive consumerism. The dreadful images I captured during my time in Manila's oldest and largest open pit dumpsite still haunt me. I pray I do not forget the people of Payatas, or forget that I am part of the reason they are forced to live on a mountain of garbage.

Saint Francis fresco, Assisi, Italy

Francis' poverty was his highest wealth; he was poor in order to possess the fullness of God and to lavish it in love on all creation and every creature God allowed to cross his path. How weightless are his wings of poverty on which his soul flew into the sunshine of true freedom. Francis, having nothing anywhere, found God everywhere. He was completely indifferent to temporal things. Yet his material poverty was nothing in comparison to his poverty of spirit. Nothing distracted him from prayer, and nothing diverted his love from God. His detachment was so great, his heart was completely emptied, leaving it undivided and available for God alone.

Those living on the margins of society, the poor, broken and rejected, are portals through which we can enter fully into the mystery of the cross.

Philadelphia, Pennsylvania

Assisi, Italy

A homeless, naked, dying man on the cross asks, Are you reasonably comfortable?

The danger of our thirst for individualism is that it weakens our awareness of the needs of others. From Christ's point of view, "you" comes before "me."

Love is service. It is the emptying of self. It is losing in order to find.

Acknowledging my own weakness increases my ability to become more merciful toward others.

Manila, the Philippines

The Old and New Testament say with one voice: To walk with the poor is to walk with God.

Tarahumara Indian Reservation, Juarez, Mexico

A *Textual Meditation*

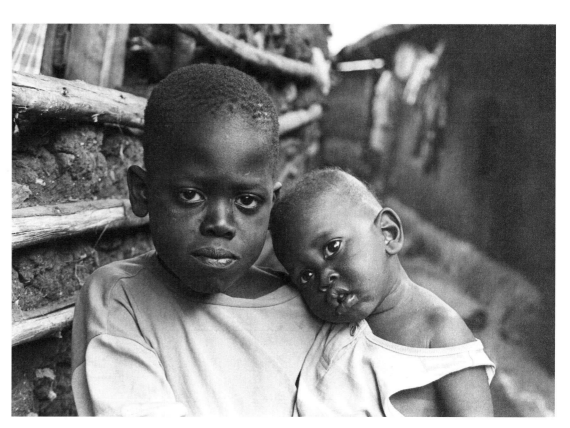

Nairobi, Kenya

You have seen the poor in these pages. What follows is meant to be a kind of *lectio divina*, or literary food for meditation.

All faiths place a strong emphasis on caring for the poor and the weak. For instance, Jesus made care for the poorest of the poor a litmus test of our love of God. As I traveled deeper and deeper into the world of severe poverty, I discovered a wide variety of voices expressing the centuries-old human struggle with poverty and how to respond to it. Following here is a sampling of collected wisdom from across the centuries and from around the world. I've gathered them into small clusters, each titled, in order to make it easier to meditate on only a few nuggets at a time.

You did not need this book to remind you that poverty exists, that there are untold numbers of people living in unimaginably horrible conditions. The growing numbers of homeless in America are on full display in every city. Most people would like to do something to ease the suffering. The sheer number of outstretched hands begging for our spare change is daunting.

But we are busy. Modern life seems hopelessly complex, requiring all of us to become master jugglers of job and family responsibilities. The demands on our time are at once maddening and frustrating. With so many things to do and so many hands stretching out for help, I think we have developed a fatigue of compassion. And when we look beyond our borders, to the dire poverty around the world, we are confounded by the need. War, famine, brutal dictatorships, natural disasters, economic recessions and corrupt governments have created a huge exodus of refugees living in squalor that defies description. We have grown weary from stories on television and in newspapers documenting the plight of the poor in Bosnia, Kenya, India, Romania, Chechnya, Zambia, Burundi, Brazil, Mexico, Haiti, Pakistan, Afghanistan, Argentina, Sri Lanka, Somalia and the Democratic Republic of Congo, to name only a handful of countries that easily spring to mind, and the cumulative effect of all the tragic stories leaves us feeling helpless to do anything about it. And so we turn away, and keep busy.

We need a new way to look at the poor and a new way to respond to the poor. We need to look through the eyes of faith, no matter what faith we follow; and we need to respond with a heart of faith. And it will not be easy. It will take time. Meditating on the plight of the poor, on the root causes of their plight, on our role in their plight and on the spiritual response to their plight, is vital. It is my prayer that this book will be but one small, first step on your journey with the poor, walking together, walking with Christ.

FROM THE OLD AND NEW TESTAMENTS

[I]f you offer your food to the hungry
and satisfy the needs of the afflicted,
then your light shall rise in the darkness
and your gloom be like the noonday.
—ISAIAH 58:10

Give some of your food to the hungry, and
some of your clothing to the naked.
—TOBIT 4:16

Bear one another's burdens, and in this way
you will fulfill the law of Christ.
—GALATIANS 6:2

ISLAMIC AND BUDDHIST TRADITIONS

Those who do not see the meaning of their life
in temporary things, in their names and bodies,
those people know the truth of life.
—*The Dhammapada* (a book of Buddhist
wisdom)

True compassion does not come from wanting
to help out those less fortunate than ourselves;
but from realizing our kinship with all things.
— PEMA CHODRON, *Start Where You Are: A*
Guide to Compassionate Living

Those who enjoin charity or justice or
reconciliation among people—whoever does
that, seeking the pleasure of God, will be given
a great reward.
—THE QUR'AN, Chapter Four, verse 114

All suffering comes from cherishing ourselves.
All happiness comes from cherishing others.
—A TIBETAN SAYING

JEWISH VOICES

There is a realm of time where the goal is not to
have but to be, not to own but to give, not to
control but to share, not to subdue but to be in
accord.— ABRAHAM JOSHUA HESCHEL, *The*
Sabbath

The justice rendered to the Other, my
neighbour, gives me an unsurpassable proximity
to God. It is as intimate as the prayer and the
liturgy which, without justice, are nothing....
—EMMANUEL LEVINAS, *Difficult Freedom: Essays*
on Judaism

For our God makes only one demand upon us.
He does not expect a humanly unattainable
completeness and perfection, but only the
willingness to do as much as we possibly can at
every single instant.
— MARTIN BUBER, *The Writings of Martin Buber*

LITERATI

Try to understand the unity of all living things.
Try to serve and suffer with all living beings.
—LEO TOLSTOY, *A Calendar of Wisdom*

The man who has begun to live more seriously
within begins to live more simply without.
—ERNEST HEMINGWAY, "True Nobility"

It is preoccupation with possessions, more than
anything else, that prevents men from living
freely and nobly. — BERTRAND RUSSELL,
Principles of Social Reconstruction

You will have found Christ when you are
concerned with other people's sufferings and not
your own.—FLANNERY O'CONNOR, from a letter

Never be proud or unkind, my dears, to any
poor man, woman or child. If they are bad,
think that they would have been better, if they
had kind friends, and good homes, and had
been better taught. So, always try to make then
better by kind persuading words....
—CHARLES DICKENS, *The Life of Our Lord*

The day that hunger is eradicated from the
earth, there will be the greatest spiritual
explosion the world has ever known. Humanity
cannot imagine the joy that will burst into the
world on the day of that great revolution.
—FEDERICO GARCIA LORCA, Spanish poet and
dramatist, 1898-1936

THE GRACE TO ACT

Many men feel frustrated, or disappointed, or even defeated, when they find themselves face to face with a situation or an evil they cannot do much about....The sense of hopelessness we all experience in such circumstances really arises from our tendency to inject too much of self into the picture. Doing so, we can easily be overwhelmed by personal feelings of inadequacy or sheer physical powerlessness, by the realization of one man's seeming insignificance in a corrupt world. We tend to concentrate on ourselves, we tend to think of what we can or cannot do, and we forget about God and his will and his providence. Yet God never forgets each individual's significance, his dignity and worth, and the role each has been asked to play in the workings of his providence. To him, each individual is equally important at all times. He cares. But he also expects each man to accept, as from his hands, the daily situations he sends him and to act as he would have him act and gives him the grace to act.
—WALTER J. CISZEK, S.J., _He Leadeth Me_

GNAWING DESPAIR

Simplicity of life and poverty are not the same. There are many people who live very simple lives, either by choice or circumstance, who are not poor. Poverty does not mean simply a lack of money or goods. In its essence, poverty means radical insecurity about the basic means of life. Poverty is literally not knowing where the next meal is coming from, or the frantic fear of getting ill because there is no money for a doctor, or the gnawing despair when one recognizes the gap between the next possible time when money will come and the actual needs of the household. It is, in short, a knowledge that the world is not solid, secure, and benign. Poverty is not only want; it is the fear and dread that derives from want.
—LAWRENCE CUNNINGHAM, _St. Francis of Assisi_

EMPTY HEARTS

It is not the man who has too little, but the man who craves more, that is poor.
— SENECA, Epistles, 2, 2

When our hearts are empty, we collect things.
—J. KRISHNAMURTI

Attachment to worldly things is a grave obstacle to those who are striving after holiness, and often brings ruin to both soul and body.
—SAINT NEILOS THE ASCETIC, _The Philokalia_, Volume One

LOVE AND COMPASSION

Compassion and love are not mere luxuries. ...compassion is one of the principal things that make our lives meaningful. It is the source of all lasting happiness and joy. And it is the foundation of a good heart, the heart of one who acts out of a desire to help others. Through kindness, through affection, through honesty, through truth and justice toward all others we ensure our own benefit. This is not a matter for complicated theorizing. It is a matter of common sense. There is no denying that consideration of others is worthwhile. There is no denying that our happiness is inextricably bound up with the happiness of others. There is no denying that if society suffers, we ourselves suffer. Nor is there any denying that the more our hearts and minds are afflicted with ill-will, the more miserable we become. Thus we can reject everything else: religion, ideology, all received wisdom. But we cannot escape the necessity of love and compassion.
—THE DALAI LAMA, _Ethics for the New Millennium_

MAHATMA GANDHI

I am part and parcel of the whole, and I cannot find God apart from the rest of humanity.

—MAHATMA GANDHI, quoted in *The Moral and Political Thought of Mahatma Gandhi* by Raghavan Naharasimhan Iyer

Gandhiji loved his people as God loved him and one of the most beautiful things that struck me about him was his non-violence and also his comparing the poor with the service of love for God. He said: "He who serves the poor serves God." Gandhiji's non-violence, I understand, is not only not using guns and bombs. It is the love and peace and compassion in our homes first. This is what spreads non-violence outside the home, if we have that love, if we have that compassion for each other. Jesus Christ said again and again: "Love one another as I have loved you."

—MOTHER TERESA, *The Joy in Loving: A Guide to Daily Living with Mother Teresa*

LEFTOVERS ARE NOT ENOUGH

True compassion is more than flinging a coin to a beggar; it is not haphazard and superficial. It comes to see that an edifice which produces beggars needs re-structuring.

— MARTIN LUTHER KING, JR., *Beyond Vietnam: A Prophecy for the '80's*

A society of genuine solidarity can be built only if the well-off, in helping the poor, do not stop at giving from what they do not need.

—POPE JOHN PAUL II, from an address on the celebration of the World Day of Peace, January 1, 1998

People lose everything they leave behind in this world; but they carry with them the rewards of charity.

—SAINT FRANCIS OF ASSISI, from the *Letter to the Faithful* (Second Version), 31

WORKS OF MERCY

We are not alone; beyond the differences that separate us, we share one common humanity and thus, belong to each other. The mystery of life is that we discover this human togetherness not when we are powerful and strong, but when we are vulnerable and weak.

—HENRI J. M. NOUWEN, *Our Greatest Gift: A Meditation on Dying and Caring*

Works of mercy are about establishing relationships. It is through the movement of grace on relationships between persons that wonderful, even miraculous, things happen.

—ROBERT SMITH, S.F.O., Personal letter

Solitude and silence may be the meat and potatoes of our prayer lives, but they are empty of nourishment when separated from service of our brothers and sisters.

—JOHN KIRVAN, *God Hunger*

LOVE YOUR NEIGHBOR

Love of our neighbor consists of three things: to desire the greater good of everyone; to do what good we can when we can; to bear, excuse and hide other's faults.— SAINT JOHN VIANNEY

You can't pray, obey, or be truly poor, says our Lord, unless you are wholly taken up with your brother's needs.—RUTH BURROWS, *Living Love*

Love itself is related more to what we do than what we say.

—SAINT IGNATIUS OF LOYOLA, *The Spiritual Exercises of St. Ignatius*

THE REAL AND CONCRETE HUMAN BEING

That's what we are here for: to make the world new. We know what to do: seek justice, love mercy, walk humbly, treat every person as though she were yourself. These are not complicated instructions. It's much harder to decipher the direction for putting together a child's tricycle than it is to understand these.
—NANCY MAIRS, *Ordinary Time: Cycles in Marriage, Faith, and Renewal*

Every time that there arises from the depths of a human heart the childish cry which Christ himself could not restrain, "Why am I being hurt?", then there is certainly injustice.
—SIMON WEIL, "Human Personality," *Two Moral Essays*

Christ did not, like a moralist, love a theory of good, but He loved the real man. He was not, like a philosopher, interested in the "universally valid," but rather in that which is of help to the real and concrete human being.
—DIETRICH BONHOEFFER, *Ethics*

SUFFERING AND COMPASSION

Sometime in your life, hope that you might see one starved man, the look on his face when the bread finally arrives. Hope that you might have baked it or bought it or even kneaded it yourself. For that look on his face, for your eyes meeting his eyes across a piece of bread, you might be willing to lose a lot, or suffer a lot, or die a little even.
—DANIEL BERRIGAN, S.J., from an address given at the College of Wooster, February, 1991

Compassion is hard because it requires the inner disposition to go with others to the place where they are weak, vulnerable, lonely, and broken. But this is not our spontaneous response to suffering. What we desire most is to do away with suffering by fleeing from it or finding a quick cure for it. As busy, active, relevant ministers, we want to earn our bread by making a real contribution. This means first and foremost doing something to show that our presence makes a difference. And so we ignore our greatest gift, which is our ability to enter into solidarity with those who suffer.
—HENRI J. M. NOUWEN, *The Way of the Heart: Desert Spirituality and Contemporary Ministry*

Suffering makes one more sensitive to the pain in the world. It can teach us to put forth a greater love for everything that exists.
—DOROTHEE SOELLE, *Suffering*, translated by Everett R. Kalin

UNBRIDLED CAPITALISM

What I am concerned about is the idolatry of the market.... Unbridled capitalism...may not be a problem for production and expansion of the economic pie, but it's a problem for human beings. It's a problem for...the realm of values and human relationships because it distorts things.
—WILLIAM BENNETT, quoted in "Capitalism Is Giddy with Triumph: Is It Possible to Overdo It?" by David Wessel and John Harwood, *The Wall Street Journal*, 14 May 1998

In losing touch with being and thus with God, we have fallen into a senseless idolatry of production and consumption for their own sakes. We have renounced the act of being and plunged ourself into process for its own sake.
—THOMAS MERTON, *Conjectures of a Guilty Bystander*

NOTHING BUT NOTHING

Outside of God there is nothing but nothing.
—MEISTER ECKHART, Sermon Thirteen

To want nothing is the only possible freedom.
—MATTHEW FOX

To come to possess all, desire the possession of nothing.
—SAINT JOHN OF THE CROSS, *The Ascent of Mount Carmel*

AN INTERDEPENDENT NETWORK

All things are interdependent.
—MEISTER ECKHART, quoted in *Original Blessing* by Matthew Fox

Injustice anywhere is a threat to justice everywhere. We are caught in an inescapable network of mutuality tied in a single garment of destiny.
—MARTIN LUTHER KING, JR., *Letter from Birmingham City Jail*

The whole idea of compassion is based on a keen awareness of the interdependence of all these living beings, which are all part of one another and all involved in one another.
—THOMAS MERTON, from a talk delivered in Bangkok, Thailand

A FOOL FOR CHRIST

I do not want to keep anything that is given to me. I want to experience hunger in order to feed the poor. I want to strip myself in order to clothe them. I want to suffer from need in order to let them enjoy plenty. Prevent people from giving me anything at all, for it is my heart's desire to run to Christ without being weighed down by burdens.
—SAINT MARGARET OF CORTONA, *The Revelations of Margaret of Cortona: The Franciscan Magdalene*

I desire and choose poverty with Christ poor rather than riches, in order to be more like Christ our Lord. Then I choose reproaches with Christ thus suffering rather than honor, and then I am willing to be considered worthless and a fool for Christ who suffered such treatment before me, rather than to be esteemed as wise and prudent in this world.
—SAINT IGNATIUS OF LOYOLA, *The Spiritual Exercises of St. Ignatius*

SMALL THINGS

Whenever you listen to someone who is suffering, you hear Christ's voice. And whenever you meet someone suffering, you meet him in person.
—DOM HELDER CAMARA, *Through the Gospel with Dom Helder Camara*

Even if you write a letter for a blind man, or you just sit and listen to someone, or you take the mail for him, or you visit somebody or bring a flower to somebody, or wash clothes for somebody or clean the house—small things, but God sees everything great.
—MOTHER TERESA, *The Joy in Loving*

A DEBT OF JUSTICE

I cannot pray if I don't serve my brother. I cannot pray to the God who incarnated himself when my brother is in need. It is an impossibility. It would be like the priest, the Levite, who passed the man beset by robbers, and that one cannot do.
—CATHERINE DE HUECK DOHERTY, *Poustinia: Christian Spirituality of the East for Western Man*

When we attend to the needs of those in want, we give them what is theirs, not ours. More than performing works of mercy, we are paying a debt of justice.
—SAINT GREGORY THE GREAT, from the *Catechism of the Catholic Church*

Whoever is spared personal pain must feel himself called to help in diminishing the pain of others.
—ALBERT SCHWEITZER, *Reverence for Life*

A WOUNDING OF THE HEART

Compassion is a wounding of the heart which love extends to all without distinction.
—JOHN RUUSBROEC, *The Spiritual Espousals and Other Works*

If you have compassion, you cannot be rich.... You can be rich only when you can bear the sight of suffering.
—THICK NHAT HANH, *The Raft Is Not The Shore*

PRECIOUS RESOURCES

The greatest injustice we have done to our poor people is that we think they are good for nothing; we have forgotten to treat them with respect, with dignity as a child of God. People have forgotten what the human touch is, what it is to smile, for somebody to smile at them, somebody to recognize them, somebody to wish them well. The terrible thing is to be unwanted.
—MOTHER TERESA, *The Joy in Loving*

We must learn to perceive "the poor" not as a problem to overcome but rather to see poor people as precious resources who have been ignored—people who have gifts and talents that will enrich the community once they are permitted as friends and neighbors into the circles of our lives.
—JIM WALLIS, editor of *Sojourners* magazine, quoted in the *Dallas Morning News*, April 24, 2001

A BIG SMILE

The man who looks prayerfully on the world is the man who does not expect happiness from himself, but who looks forward toward the other who is coming. It is often said that a man who prays is conscious of his dependence, and in his prayer he expresses his helplessness.
—HENRI J.M. NOUWEN, *With Open Hands*

It is not how much we really "have" to give but how empty we are—so that we can receive fully in our life. Take away your eyes from yourself and rejoice that you have nothing—that you are nothing—that you can do nothing. Give Jesus a big smile each time your nothingness frightens you.—MOTHER TERESA, *The Joy in Loving*

The alternative to poverty is not wealth but justice, and relationships of fellowship. Poverty and wealth are expressions of a sick and dehumanized society.
—LEONARDO BOFF, *The Path to Hope*

POVERTY OF THE HEART

Homelessness is not only of bricks but homelessness comes from that terrible loneliness that the unwanted, the unloved know along their way. Are we there? Do we know them? Do we see them?...When I pick up a hungry person from the street, I give him a plate of rice, a piece of bread. But a person who is shut out, who feels unwanted, unloved, terrified, the person who has been thrown out of society— that spiritual poverty is much harder to overcome.... The greatest poverty in the world is not the want of food but the want of love. You have the poverty of people who are dissatisfied with what they have, who do not know how to suffer, who give in to despair. The poverty of the heart is often more difficult to relieve and to defeat.
—MOTHER TERESA, *The Joy in Loving*

A LIVING FLAME

The great activity of our life is to love. I see God as one act—just loving, like the sun always shining.
—ALFRED BOEDDEKER, O.F.M., quoted in *The Man Behind the Miracle: The Story of Alfred Boeddeker, O.F.M.*, by Madeline Hartman

[W]e should love God because he is God and … the measure of our love should be to love him without measure.
—SAINT BERNARD OF CLAIRVAUX, *The Love of God*

He is truly great who is great in charity.
—THOMAS À KEMPIS, *Imitation of Christ*, Pt. I, ch. 3

Charity for the poor is like a living flame; the drier the fuel, the brighter it burns. In your service to the poor do not give only your hands but also yours hearts. Charity to be fruitful must cost us. Give until it hurts. To love, it is necessary to give: to give it is necessary to be free from selfishness.
—MOTHER TERESA, *The Joy in Loving*

WALKING WITH THE POOR

With the means available today, poverty, hunger and disease can no longer be regarded as either normal or inevitable.
—POPE JOHN PAUL II, from an address to the Food and Agriculture Organization of the United Nations, November 18, 1999

A Church that does not unite itself to the poor in order to renounce—from the place of the poor—the injustice committed against them is not truly the Church of Jesus Christ.
—ARCHBISHOP OSCAR ROMERO, *The Violence of Love*, translated by James R. Brockman

When I give food to the poor, they call me a saint. When I asked why the poor have no food, they call me a communist.
—DOM HELDER CAMARA, *Sister Earth: Creation, Ecology, and the Spirit*

REAL LOVE

I am thinking more and more that God will not judge us either for the good or the evil that we have done, but simply for whether we have been capable of accepting God's love and transmitting it to other people.
—PEDRO CASALDÁLIGA, Bishop of Brazil, from *Mystic of Liberation* by Teofilo Cabestrero

Love to be real, it must cost—it must hurt—it must empty us of self.
—MOTHER TERESA, from *Works of Love Are Works of Peace* by Michael Collopy

To ease another's heartbreak is to forget one's own.—MALCOLM MUGGERIDGE

SHELL OF SELFISHNESS

Break through your shell of selfishness.
If you do not
know yourself,
you will never know
others.
Selfishness
is the deepest root
of all unhappiness
—your own and
—that of the whole world.
It feeds an insatiable hunger
that first eats up
everything belonging to others
and then causes a creature
to devour itself.
—DOM HELDER CAMARA, *Hoping Against All Hope*

A HAPPY SMILE

Superficial desires—such as those linked with consumerism—demonstrate all too graphically our cultural narcissism, but authentic desires always lead us out of ourselves and into the human community.

—E. EDWARD KINERK, S.J., "Eliciting Great Desires: Their Place in the Spirituality of the Society of Jesus," *Studies in the Spirituality of Jesuits* XVI:5 (November 1984)

Be kind and merciful. Let no one ever come to you without leaving better and happier. Be a living expression of God's kindness: kindness in your face, kindness in your eyes, kindness in your smile, kindness in your warm greeting. To children, to the poor, to all who suffer and are lonely, give always a happy smile. Give then not only your care but also your heart.

—MOTHER TERESA, *The Joy in Loving*

SPIRITUAL POVERTY

Poverty is the queen of virtues.

—SAINT FRANCIS OF ASSISI, *Prayer of Saint Francis of Assisi to Obtain the Grace of Poverty*

Spiritual poverty is complete dispassion; when the intellect has reached this state it abandons all worldly things.

—SAINT THALASSIOS, *The Philokalia*

To be without desire is a mark of poverty. At the moment I am surrounded by people who cling to their desires, so much so that they haven't any interest for others: they give up listening, and are incapable of loving their neighbor.

—DIETRICH BONHOEFFER, *Letters and Papers from Prison*

THE FRUIT OF LOVE

It is not how much you give, but with how much love you give it.

—MOTHER TERESA

God is love and if we live in union with God, we have the strength and longing to love others. Service is a spiritual activity, the natural fruit of love. God, who is love, is ever serving and caring for Creation. Human beings are made to be like God and so they too should never tire of serving others.

—SUNDAR SINGH, *Wisdom of the Sadhu*

A CHILD OF GOD

You are a rich nation but on your streets I saw a man lying drunk and no one picked him up, no one seemed to bother about him, no one tried to restore to him his human dignity, to bring back to him the sense that he is a brother, a child of God.

—MOTHER TERESA, *The Joy in Loving*

Be thou jealous of thine own self when thou seest that it is at ease and thy fellow in distress, that it is in high estate and he is brought low, that it is at rest and he is at labour. Make thine own self lose its pleasures and bear the sorrow of its fellows.

—SAUTIDEVA, quoted by Thomas Merton, *The Other Side of the Mountain: The End of the Journey* (Journals of Thomas Merton, Volume 7 1967-1968)

GUESTS AT YOUR TABLE

If you only want to have more and more, if your idol is profit and pleasure, remember that man's value is not measured by what he has, but by what he is. So let him who has accumulated a great deal, and who thinks that everything is summed up in this, remember that he may be worth far less (within himself and in the eyes of God) than any of those poor and unknown persons.

—POPE JOHN PAUL II, Address to Indians of Amazonia, June 30, 1980

The poor in the United States and of the world are your brothers and sisters in Christ. You must never be content to leave them just the crumbs from the feast. You must take of your substance, and not just of your abundance, in order to help them. And you must treat them like guests at your family table.

—POPE JOHN PAUL II, Homily at Mass at Yankee Stadium, New York, October 2, 1979

One of the greatest injustices in the contemporary world consists precisely of this: that the ones who possess much are relatively few and those who possess almost nothing are many. It is the injustice of the poor distribution of the goods and services originally intended for all.

—POPE JOHN PAUL II, *On Social Concerns (Sollicitudo rei socialis)*, 1987

A CUP OF WATER

Do you want to honor Christ? Then do not scorn him in his nakedness, nor honor him here in the church with silken garments while neglecting him outside where he is cold and naked…. Of what use is it to weigh down Christ's table with golden cups, when he himself is dying of hunger? First, fill him when he is hungry; then use the means you have left to adorn his table. Will you have a golden cup made but not give a cup of water? What is the use of providing the table with cloths woven of gold thread, and not providing Christ himself with the clothes he needs?

—SAINT JOHN CHRYSOSTOM, from a homily on the Gospel of Matthew

BREAD FOR THE WORLD

God requires more from us than charity. God requires justice.

—DAVID BECKMANN, president of Bread for the World, Silver Springs, Maryland, from an interview with the author on December 8, 1999

Jesus spent a lot of time disobeying and working against laws that squeezed and marginalized people….All of us pay for widespread hunger—in violence, disease, lost economic opportunity and social tension.

—DAVID BECKMANN, Interview with the author

THE PLACES OF THE POOR

Jesus was not a liar. When he said, "I was hungry and you fed me," he was declaring God's eternal solidarity with all those persons for whom to live means to suffer. He was stating with stark simplicity that the tender and merciful love of God is always approachable, always humble, and always waiting with pregnant anticipation our arrival at the places of the poor, and then the discovery of our own poverty in their hearts.

—ROBERT SMITH, S.F.O., The Franciscan Workers of Junipero Serra Community, Salinas, California

THE TAIL OF A MOUSE

As long as individuals serve their own personal interests, the common good will suffer.
—DESIDERIUS ERASMUS

Men pray to the Almighty to relieve poverty. But poverty comes not from God's laws—it is blasphemy of the worst kind to say that. Poverty comes from man's injustice to his fellow man.—LEO TOLSTOY

If you are neutral in situations of injustice, you have chosen the side of the oppressor. If an elephant has his foot on the tail of a mouse and you say you are neutral, the mouse will not appreciate your neutrality.—DESMOND TUTU

THE ECONOMY OF DIVINE CHARITY

A happiness that is sought for ourselves alone can never be found: for a happiness that is diminished by being shared is not big enough to make us happy…. True happiness is found in unselfish love, a love which increases in proportion as it is shared.
—THOMAS MERTON, *No Man Is an Island*

In the economy of divine charity we have only as much as we give. But we are called upon to give as much as we have, and more: as much as we are. So the measure of our love is theoretically without limit. The more we desire to give ourselves in charity, the more charity we will have to give. And the more we give the more truly we shall be. For the Lord endows us with a being proportionate to the giving for which we are destined.
—THOMAS MERTON, *No Man Is an Island*

No man who ignores the rights and needs of others can hope to walk in the light of contemplation, because his way has turned aside from truth, from compassion, and therefore from God. The obstacle is in our "self," that is to say in the tenacious need to maintain our separate, external, egocentric will.
—THOMAS MERTON, *New Seeds of Contemplation*

A DISTRESSING DISGUISE

I never look at the masses as my responsibility. I look only at the individual. I can love only one person at a time. I can feed only one person at a time.

Just one, one, one….

The whole work is only a drop in the ocean. But if we don't put the drop in, the ocean would be one drop less.

Same thing for you. Same thing in your family. Same thing in the church where you go. Just begin…one, one, one.

At the end of our lives, we will not be judged by how many diplomas we have received, how much money we have made or how many great things we have done. We will be judged by "I was hungry and you gave me to eat. I was naked and you clothed me. I was homeless and you took me in."

Hungry not only for clothing—but hungry for love. Naked not only for clothing—but naked for human dignity and respect.

Homeless not only for want of a room of bricks—but homeless because of rejection.

This is Christ in distressing disguise.
—MOTHER TERESA, as quoted by Andrew Harvey, editor, in *The Essential Mystics: The Soul's Journey into Truth*

241

DAVID BECKMAN

Rev. David Beckmann is president of
Bread for the World, a Christian
citizens' movement against hunger.
Gerard Thomas Straub is a member
of the board of directors. For more
information on how you can get
involved in Bread for the World's
work for hungry people,
call 800-82-BREAD or visit
www.bread.org. A list of other
organizations that work to end
poverty is available at
www.bread.org/links.html

We Don't Have to Be Saints to Make a Difference

I KNOW HOW YOU FEEL. I've felt strongly about hunger and poverty in our world for a long time. I was taught about God's love for me—and for people in need—at an early age. I went to college in the 1960s, and the civil rights and antiwar movements of that time made me more aware of injustice. I spent time in Asia, Africa and Latin America and developed relationships with some very poor people. Now I'm the president of Bread for the World, a grassroots anti-hunger lobbying group in Washington, D.C.

And it still gets to me—the reality of hunger and poverty. The fact that nearly 800 million people in the world don't have enough to eat, even today when the richest people in the world are the richest anyone has ever been in the history of humankind. So many of God's children aren't able to live full and productive lives because they are poor. It makes me angry. It makes me sad. It makes me determined to change things. I believe the persistence of unnecessary poverty is the most morally scandalous aspect of our world.

Hunger and poverty can be over-whelming. They can incapacitate us. Our guilt and impotence can cause us to blame the victims or turn away and do nothing. Live our lives as if we haven't seen our brothers and sisters in need.

Maybe you bought this book because the pictures caught your attention. Or perhaps someone gave it to you because they thought your heart would be moved by the images captured by Gerry's camera. Whatever the reason, now you have seen the life reality of millions of poor people on this planet.

The question is what are you going to do about it?

In my life journey, I've ended up as the head of a 45,000-member Christian anti-hunger organization. But I'm no Mother Teresa. My family is affluent. I could do much more for poor people than I do.

But we don't have to be saints to make a difference. Everything we do, no matter how small, is important. The Bible teaches us that we need only faith the size of a mustard seed to move mountains. For Christians, this idea is simple: Open the door a crack and God's justice can break through. The living God is on the side of life and healing. God works to overthrow injustice—while patiently suffering alongside us, forgiving us and granting us another chance every day.

Whether you are Christian or not, you can be part of the solution. You don't have to get your own life perfectly in order before you're able to help. Just take a step. Every act makes a difference, be it tutoring a child, giving money to a charity or volunteering in a soup kitchen. All are helpful to those in need, one person at a time.

In the United States, we have another amazing opportunity to help: our citizenship. We live in the richest, most powerful country in the world, and our government is a democracy. Our political leaders make decisions that can mean the difference between life and death for millions of hungry and poor people around the world. Economic and social policy, both domestic and international, can provide people with tools to pull themselves out of poverty, or it can reinforce systems that make it nearly impossible for them to escape. One bill in the U.S. Congress can mean improved agricultural training and education throughout Africa so local farmers can grow food for their families. Another bill can slash the Food Stamp Program and take food off the tables of millions of working, low-income American families.

We can change individual situations through charity, and we can change whole systems through democracy. We can change the way the world works so hungry and poor people are no longer so completely disregarded and trampled by the rest of the world. I believe God looks at our rich and powerful nation and asks how we will respond to hungry and poor people. How would the world be different if our elected leaders had the same question at the forefront when making policy decisions?

For the first time in history, we have the knowledge, resources and technology to end widespread, routine hunger. The costs would be minimal—a tiny percentage of the U.S. government's annual budget. What's needed is a modest change in national priorities. Once again, it doesn't take much. You don't have to be a policy expert. You don't have to be a political junkie. You just have to care.

Elaine Van Cleave, a friend of mine and a member of Bread for the World, did just that. She went to Washington and asked her member of Congress to support a bill that would help hungry people in Africa. He was a conservative who had never been to Africa and who typically didn't support this kind of legislation. But she appealed to him on a level we can all appreciate: that of a mother.

"Every day, 30,000 children die in the developing world, half from hunger-related causes," she told him. "As a mother, that just kills me. Most of the time, I feel like I can't do anything about it. The problem is too big. But this bill would help."

Her representative introduced the bill. He became a forceful, influential advocate himself. The bill passed. It won billions of dollars in lifesaving provisions for Africa.

Elaine wasn't an expert in policy. She just cares. Just like you.

You don't have to fly to Washington to influence your members of Congress. Write a letter. Send an E-mail. Make a phone call. Visit your senators and representative when they're at home in your state. Tell them that you care about hungry people and ask them to take specific action. U.S. citizens have enormous power to influence change.

Working with Bread for the World has shown me that a small group of people can make a big difference for hungry and poor people. Year after year, I witness unexpected miracles taking place on Capitol Hill. Concerned citizens open the door and God's justice bursts through.

Hunger has declined in the past twenty-five years. There is still much more to be done, as evidenced by the stirring images in this book. Yet, I am gripped by tremendous hope. In this time of remarkable blessing, we can make progress against poverty. Hunger doesn't have to be routine.

When the prophet Isaiah received a vision from God, it felt like a coal in his mouth. The images in this book are like hot coal—a burning word that must be spoken. Isaiah felt inadequate to see the vision he was given. Few of us feel up to the job of turning the course of history. But the angel who touched the coal to Isaiah's lips assured him that God would use him, despite his shortcomings, to deliver a world-shaking message to his neighbors and nation.

Gerry wrote this book. Bread for the World members talk to their members of Congress.

Now it's your turn. What are you going to do?

President and CEO of Union Rescue
Mission in Los Angeles, California

IT'S THE EYES. Look closely at the eyes in these photos. Look carefully again into the eyes of your loved ones. Look for the first time, really, at the eyes of a homeless person. Then let your mind blur the hair color, the skin color, the quality or style of the clothing they are wearing and—I believe—you will see what God sees. Yes, the eyes are windows to the soul. And when you look into another's they are also a mirror image of you.

I have had the profound privilege of looking into the eyes of people in the lines at our door, which flow out into the streets of Los Angeles. They are homeless veterans, women escaping an abusive partner, men wrestling with a long debilitating addiction…and, unfortunately, innocent children by the hundreds displaced by cruel circumstance through no fault of their own. And those eyes are saying exactly the same thing that I have seen in the eyes of a child in Capetown, South Africa; Cluj, Romania; Lhasa, Tibet or one of the other 90

countries in which I have worked and traveled. We each need to be loved and affirmed. We each want to be engaged in meaningful and sustaining endeavors and relationships. We each strive for a relative state of security, shelter and sustenance for our well-being.

Since we are not God, and therefore do not transcend the barriers that separate us, every one of us screens the experiences of life through a certain filter, a particular worldview. We are each, after all, the sum total of our genetic heritage and our necessarily limiting environments. It is impossible for us to have lived in all circumstances. And while I claim a certain faith, and have by this time in my life determined what philosophical constructs I believe in, the concept of the commonality of humankind and the universality of our suffering have always remained too ethereal and detached for me—simply too abstract. Seriously, how much in common do you feel with a homeless person who comes to wash

your windshield against your wishes, or with a bearded warrior in some distant land on the evening news?

But over time I have come to understand something most profound. I am, in fact, no different in my desires or more highly esteemed by God, than anyone else. This journey started by looking past the face into the eyes. It continued as I made time, made myself available to volunteer for a work project or a mission trip. And then as I began to see deep joy in those who had nothing but each other, who recognized the want in my own life of abundance and yet reached out to me. When I was a younger man, I recall making assumptions about the motivation or decisions of my superiors at work. Now that I am a CEO I have, if you will, a redemptive understanding of what that boss had to live through to function in his role. When I was a younger man I recall making value judgments about a person because of their speech pattern or level of hygiene. Now that I have begun to see the relationship of poverty to injustice and my own participation in both, I have a direct flesh and blood experience, an incarnational understanding, of what a homeless person feels like when she looks back at me. Of course, I have read about the redemptive and the incarnational in my own faith tradition. But it wasn't until I understood my own void that I discovered how to fill it—in service to others.

It's funny, isn't it, that we labor hard to prevent ourselves from lacking. We acquire and save, but then we start to capture and withhold that which God has intended for us to share. Money—yes, if we have any—but I am especially talking about ourselves, our time. It isn't until we encounter a crucible experience, a place of pain where someone reached out to us at our lowest place of hopelessness, that we fully understand the eternal significance of seeing one who is hungry—and then doing something about it.

One of those crucible experiences for me was the death of my oldest daughter Bristol Michelle at age 10 after a debilitating terminal illness. From a beautiful blonde, blue-eyed, "normal" two-year-old, she died a twisted mess with acute scoliosis, went blind and deaf and could not talk. On the night after she died, I sat down at my desk with red eyes and a massive headache and wrote her one last letter to express my feelings. One portion of that letter reads, "Bristol, I loved you when I was close to God and when He seemed far away; when I was full of faith and also when I was angry at Him. And the reason I loved you, my Bristol, in spite of these difficulties, is that God put this love in my heart. This is the wondrous nature of God's love, that he loves us even when we are blind, deaf, or twisted—in body or in spirit. God loves us even when we can't tell Him that we love Him back."

When we look into the eyes of another, we can truly see the heart of God. And then there is no question what we need to do.

PART FOUR

The Photographer's Journal

Manila, the Philippines

This book has been heavy in images and ideas. But now that we have reached the end of the book, we are left with one burning question: What do we do? More importantly: What do I do?

And with that difficult question, we begin our real journey with the poor.

As I write these words, it is the first Sunday of Advent; we are in the final weeks of 2001, a truly tumultuous year, a year which has seen the globe littered with victims of violence, hatred, terrorism and social injustice, making the problem of hunger and severe poverty even worse than it was before I took the first photograph. The first trip I made for this book was to India; I landed in Calcutta on October 26, 1999. Even after more than two full years of being with the poor and thinking about poverty from economic, social and spiritual perspectives, carefully examining both the varied causes and the suggested solutions, the very question of what do I do still takes my breath away, still leaves me nearly paralyzed by indecision and a fear of my own ineffectiveness. David Beckmann has offered a possible suggestion. But I feel ill-equipped to tell you, dear reader, what to do. As I reflected on my journey with the poor, I have been better able to formulate an answer for myself, and have also learned a little something about the role of faith not only in my life but in my response to the poor.

My personal reflection was made a bit easier because I had been keeping a journal since that first trip to India. Because I am a writer, it was quite natural for me to document my travels, impressions and thoughts. Because the making of this book—the taking of the photographs, the talking with the poor, the writing of the text—was such a personal endeavor, it may be that a small portion of the entries from my journal—chosen mainly from those made in India and Kenya—not only will make a fitting end to the book but also will help you to begin your own personal journey with the poor.

A RESTLESS NIGHT IN CALCUTTA

The plane's wheels touched down in Calcutta at 10:46 in the evening. With stops in Taipei and Singapore, it had been a long, grueling trip from Los Angeles—consuming a total of twenty hours on planes and ten hours between flights. I was exhausted, yet filled with excitement at being in India. I had no idea of what I was about to see and experience, no idea of the rough road ahead, a road that would be challenging physically, emotionally and spiritually. The plane came to a stop a short distance from the terminal. As I looked out the window into the darkness, I felt a trace of anxiety...I was about to step into the unknown.

At the foot of the steps, soldiers with rifles directed the passengers to a dilapidated old bus. The driver seemed to have a difficult time starting the engine and an even more difficult time shifting into first gear, and when the bus finally lunged forward, the engine sounded like an aged washing machine. After driving only a few yards, the bus stopped in front of the international arrivals building. I wondered why we could not have walked the short distance. The dimly lit interior of the building looked as if it had not been painted in thirty years. There were no custom forms on the plane, and so everyone scrambled to find the appropriate form and a flat surface on which to write. I had been in India less than fifteen minutes and I already knew that the gulf between my safe, comfortable life in Los Angeles and life in India was enormous. I could sense the anxiety turning to fear even before I left the airport.

After passing through customs, I was greeted by Father Gearóid Francisco Ó Conaire, O.F.M. The tall, handsome friar from Ireland was easy to spot, as he towered over the crowd of people waiting for passengers to emerge from customs. His broad smile soothed my anxiety. Francisco worked as a missionary in El Salvador for fifteen years before being assigned to the Office of Justice, Peace and the Integrity of Creation in the Franciscan curia in Rome. He arrived in Calcutta a few hours before me. He was about to embark on a tour of Franciscan friaries in six cities in India, and I was tagging along to learn about poverty. Real poverty.

We walked to a line of very old taxis.

From a distance, I thought they were part of some display showcasing British cars from the early 1950s. For a guy from Hollywood, everything seems like a movie prop. We got in one, and I quickly realized this was no movie. This was real life. A spring protruded through a hole in the back seat upon which my back seat rested. The taxi seemed on the verge of falling apart. The driver could not start the engine. He got out and shouted to some pals who rushed over and began pushing the car until it reached sufficient speed for the driver to pop the clutch, which managed to get the engine to start.

At first, Francisco and I were consumed with travel stories about our long journeys and the itinerary ahead of us. But as we approached the city, my attention was increasingly drawn out the window. The streets were lined with homeless people. Every inch of the sidewalks was covered with sleeping bodies. I saw one young boy, perhaps five years old, sleeping naked on the ground. The closer we came to the city, the more intense the scene became. We drove past decayed buildings and people standing around large fires burning in barrels. The streets became more and more congested.

Cows and wild dogs shared the road with cars, antiquated trucks and twenty-foot-long ox-drawn carts hauling bamboo trees. Sidewalks were covered with bodies buried under old blankets. The drive was draining me of words and emotions. I sat in stunned silence.

The taxi drove through a short, dingy tunnel taking us under the main road. The narrow tunnel was so crowded with pedestrians that the taxi could barely move. The glass window was the only thing separating me from the mass of tormented humanity. I could see their faces, their pain. We emerged from the tunnel into a densely congested maze of streets so jammed with people and vehicles that the taxi frequently came to a complete stop. People were cooking on open fires along the curb. A truck backed into the taxi. The driver got out to inspect the damage. The headlight had been smashed. The taxi became engulfed in a sea of people. Many looked at us through the window. I felt vulnerable, naked. I had a big bag in the trunk loaded with two weeks' worth of clothes. Many of the people outside the taxi were nearly naked. On my lap, I clutched my camera bag containing a 35-mm camera and a digital video camera whose combined value was around $7,000—more money than all these people would see in a lifetime. Francisco said the people live on less than a dollar a day. I had twenty years of income in my camera bag. Reality was slapping me in the face. The stench and sound were overpowering. The streets vibrated with a constant noise, a painful wail. I was frightened. I thought that if my wife knew how dangerous this trip was she would kill me. I wondered what the hell I was doing here.

After worming our way through the streets for about fifteen minutes, the taxi stopped and Father Francisco said, "We're home." In stunned disbelief, I responded, "We're home? Where are we? We're nowhere!" I could not believe we were getting out of the taxi. We walked to the back of the car to get my big, fat bag from the trunk. I felt like an idiot carrying so much stuff past so many people who had so little. We squeezed our way onto the sidewalk. People sat on the ground, backs against a sheet metal fence. Francisco pounded on the fence. Shortly thereafter,

the fence slowly shifted apart, and we walked into the courtyard of an old church. I learned that we were staying here tonight, the guests of two diocesan priests. An elderly Indian man led us up a flight of rickety stairs along the outside of the building and into a room on the second floor of the rectory. The priests had retired for the evening, and so we were confined to our room.

The dusty, dark room was empty, except for two wooden pallets on the floor, each with a very thin, straw mattress. The bathroom, lit by a single, naked light bulb, was filthy and had fifty-year-old plumbing. The toilet leaked all over the concrete floor when you flushed it. A noisy overhead fan had little effect on the hot, heavy night air, but it did circulate the air enough to make it more difficult for the mosquitoes to land on you. There was a poster tacked to one wall: *Change your thoughts and you will change the world*. It was going to take a lot more than changed thoughts to fix what I had seen in less than ninety minutes in India.

Francisco lay down and within minutes he was sound asleep. Sure, he has been to the worst slums on earth. He was used to this. To me, it was a nightmare. I lay silently

on the pallet all night, never falling asleep. My mind was too busy trying to sort out all I had seen. What am I doing here? What can one person do? The problem is overwhelming. I thought of my safe, quiet home in Los Angeles, where I am surrounded by my books and music and films and walls covered with art. The contrast to this stark room was hard to process. I could hear the constant clamor from the streets. It never became quiet. Dogs barked. Kids cried. Men shouted. I tried to blot out the worst word in human language—*hopeless*—by constantly repeating, "Lord Jesus Christ, have mercy on me, a sinner."

At six in the morning, the church bells rang, briefly bringing a sense of peace to the chaos within me and outside the fence. After breakfast, we were going to Mother Teresa's home for the dying. I wanted to go back to the airport and catch the next flight to anywhere in the United States.

You can see pictures of this kind of poverty and suffering on TV or in books, and while they are able to convey some of the emotion, it is impossible for any photograph to hit as hard as the taxi ride from the airport. Before landing, the airline had played a video depicting India and its exotic, exciting tourist attractions. We saw wealthy people climbing the majestic Himalayas and white-water rafting down crystal-clear rivers. We saw safaris, food, culture, history and famous landmarks, such as the Taj Mahal—but we saw no poor, no mind-numbing poverty. At the airport in Singapore, I had bought a copy of the *International Herald Tribune* because I wanted to see how the New York Yankees did in the second game of the World Series. Now, as I lay in the darkness of our room in Calcutta, my concern over whether or not the Yankees will win the series seems ludicrous. We love diversion, shun reality. We live in an illusion. But I could not ignore the reality outside the rectory: sidewalks littered with sleeping people, naked children, bugs, disease, open sewers and the unbearable stench of hopelessness.

And it looked worse in daylight.

At the tomb of Mother Teresa, I scribbled down these thoughts:

Jesus was born in poverty and simplicity.
  How can I reject or dishonor the
  birthplace of my savior?
God, whose richness knows no limitation,

has chosen to enter into our poverty.
When we realize the emptiness of all material
  things, we are free to encounter God.
When I am busy providing for my own
  security, I am not free to be sensitive to
  the needs of others.
Greed is a death sentence to the spirit.
Security outside of God is a dream.

A LEISURELY, HOT SHOWER

The friary in Guwahati (in Northern India) has no indoor plumbing, which means no toilet, no shower. The "bathroom" is a small room. There is a hole in the concrete floor into which you deposit your waste material. You flush by pouring water down the hole. In one corner there are five large plastic barrels filled with water. The water is hauled in buckets from the well outside the house. You "shower" by using a small scoop to pour the water—the cold water—over your body. As I "showered" this morning, I realized how much water the average American consumes each day during long, leisurely, hot showers.

Last night when I was in the process of figuring out how to deposit my waste into

the hole, I spotted a snake slithering down the wall. I may not go to the bathroom again until I get home.

Yesterday we met a young girl, maybe twelve or thirteen years old, who was sold to a family to clean their house. Tomorrow we travel by bus—a three-hour trip—to Rangjuli, an isolated hamlet (not far from the border of Bhutan) in an area of great political unrest. Last week, the friars who minister to the tribal people living in clusters of straw huts were robbed at gunpoint.

A LUCKY MAN

Shortly before ten o'clock in the morning on February 10, 2000, I was standing in front of St. Boniface Church in the Tenderloin section of San Francisco when a flash of insight danced across my perplexed mind. High clouds framed the bell tower of the church creating a beautiful image...an image in stark contrast to the harshness of life on the streets of this rough-and-tumble neighborhood, which is anything but tender. I was feeling a bit down, overcome by the magnitude of the problem of homelessness in America.

My travels through India, the Philippines and Mexico had brought me face to face with some staggering levels of poverty. The horrors of the slums in Calcutta, Manila and Juarez defy imagination. The garbage dumps of Payatas still haunt me. Yet, my days in San Francisco were somehow more disheartening—and I could not figure out why.

I struggled to recall something Mother Teresa once said about the poverty in the United States being far worse than that of India, a statement that sounded absurd after spending time in India. But as I walked the streets of San Francisco, I found myself nodding in agreement with Mother Teresa's observation.

In Third World countries, the poverty is primarily material. People have nothing, lacking even the barest essentials for life. In San Francisco, the poverty, which rubs up against an abundance of riches, goes far beyond material poverty. Here there is an unhealthy, debilitating poverty of spirit. Alcohol, drugs, mental illness, violence and a sense of complete rejection by society have robbed many of the street people of any sense of hope, any sense of normalcy, any sense of dignity. They wander the streets in filthy clothes, begging as they shuffle along among the various places that offer a meal or a bed or medical assistance. They endure cold nights, rainy days, sore feet, long lines...and disdainful glances from people with a place to go, hurrying home or to work. Worse than being homeless, they are worthless.

In the places in India, the Philippines and Mexico I had visited, I saw some signs of joy and hope in the chronically poor. I saw smiles, I felt warmth in the midst of deep material depravation. On the streets of San Francisco, I encountered anger and hatred. One homeless woman spat on a Franciscan friar who was wearing his habit. Racial tension rippled through the air. Guns and knives were hidden under the rags they wore. I saw homeless people fighting with each other over a spot to sit or a place in line. I found myself becoming depressed. I never felt depressed in India or the Philippines or Mexico; in those places, I mainly felt shock and horror at the conditions in which people where forced to live.

As I looked up at the cloud-framed bell tower of the nearly hundred-year-old church with a long history of reaching out to the poorest of the poor, I suddenly realized I was a lucky man. Lucky because I knew beyond a shadow of doubt that God was real and loved me beyond measure...even though I had done nothing to deserve God's unconditional and unlimited love. The reason the poor people in the Tenderloin section of this beautiful city by the bay are so sad and hopeless is that they do not have any experience of love. Instead, they are used and abused, neglected and rejected. Instead of the warmth of love, they feel the coldness of isolation and loneliness.

If I lost all the material things in my life—my home, my cherished possessions—I would still have the love of God and the love of my wife to enrich my life. No one could rob me of the divine and human love that was mine. The real poverty of the people of the Tenderloin is a lack of love. Many of the street people bear the scars of physical and mental abuse, of growing up unwanted and unloved. Their anger and hatred is certainly understandable.

I have no idea how to fix—or even

ease—the plight of the homeless. All I know is that they need far more than a handout, far more than a hot meal and a warm bed...they need love. Only God, whose love carries no conditions nor has no limits, can teach us how to love those we think, in our human weakness, are unlovable. I was repelled by many of the people I saw on the streets of San Francisco. I would have a hard time embracing the woman who spit on the friar.

It is easy for me to love God and my wife, but I must learn to love when it hurts.

But how?

Perhaps by taking one small step at a time, beginning with offering the homeless person some tangible gesture of kindness...a simple smile that acknowledges the divinity within each person.

God wants us to use more than our hands in helping the homeless, wants us to do more than give them a meal or a blanket. We must become God's arms, embracing the rejected, in order for them to feel the reality of God's love.

WHAT NO ONE ELSE CAN DO

About four months into this project, I was weighed down by the enormity of what I had undertaken. After visiting more than half a dozen cities in India, two cities in the Philippines and a handful of cities in the United States, I had already spent a considerable amount of my own money and seemed miles from my goal. And I was no closer to understanding the problem of poverty. I was riddled with doubts and felt lost. After looking at the first fifty or so pictures I had selected from the thousands I had taken, a friend said, "Who would want to buy a book of pictures of poor people?"

The question stunned me.

I had not thought about the marketability of the book I was writing. I was writing it because I felt compelled to write it.

The idea of marrying words to images in a book exploring material poverty and poverty of spirit seemed to me to have been inspired by God. I felt ordained by God to pick up my camera and pen and portray poverty, using Saint Francis of Assisi as my guide.

Yet, I was suddenly on the verge of abandoning my "calling." My biggest excuse was lack of funding. I was unable to trust God to supply me with what I needed in order to do the task God had given to me. Then one day I came across these words from the pen of Dorothy Day.

> God expects something from each one of us that no one else can do. If we don't do it, it will not be done.

I vowed to continue. And in the months to come, the money necessary for travel and other expenses seemingly appeared out of the blue—with the help of many people.

God had given me something to do that no one else could do—or at least wanted to do. And God gave me the means to do it.

If you are wondering what you can do, I would suggest you do what God asks you to do...do what you alone can do. And the only way of discerning what God is asking of you is to try to maintain a spirit of prayerfulness throughout the day.

A GRUELING TRIP

Saturday, May 13, 2000—North Hollywood. I leave early tomorrow morning for Nairobi, Kenya. A taxi will pick me up at 5:30 a.m. to whisk me to Los Angeles Airport. From there I'll go to Minneapolis, then to Amsterdam, and arrive in Nairobi at 8:15 p.m. Monday night. This will be a grueling trip, with a total of twenty-three hours of flying time on the three flights.

Confession: I am nervous about this trip. Tour books paint the picture of idyllic safaris, wild animals under wide-open skies in Kenya. What I have found surfing the Internet presents a far different picture. Crime in Nairobi abounds, touching nearly everyone. Nearly half the population is unemployed. Government and police corruption is widespread. Power outages are commonplace. The infrastructure is crumbling. Illness from tainted food is a constant threat.

I am tired before I even begin the trip, worn down by all my travel this year and emotionally drained from all the suffering I have seen. I am nervous about my own safety. I dread seeing the levels of poverty I am sure to encounter in the slums I will be visiting.

No one seems to understand what I am doing. At times, I don't understand it. Who wants to see pictures of slums? I do not know; I only know I feel compelled to take them and to try to understand what I have seen. God led Saint Francis into the arms of the poor so he could embrace and be embraced by them. I am still trying to figure out Saint Francis' love of poverty and why he opted to live and work among the poor.

None of it makes any sense. This trip—the photo/essay book—is simply an exercise in faith.

ONLY DANGEROUS AT NIGHT

May 15, 2000—11:35 p.m., Nairobi, Kenya. I was greeted at the airport by Brother Frederick, a friar whom I had met a few years back at Collegio Sant' Isidoro in Rome. As we drove along a darkened, lonely stretch of road after leaving the airport, Frederick told me a story that confirmed my fears about Nairobi. He said a few nights ago some Missionary Sisters of Charity, dressed in the habits made famous by their founder, Mother Teresa, were driving a visitor to the airport. Suddenly, they had to stop their car because of two flat tires. When the sisters emerged from the car, they were forced to the ground by a gang of thugs, who robbed them and their visitor at gunpoint. The thugs had spread nails and other debris on the road that punctured the sisters' tires. Wow...if they could rob Sisters of Charity, what the heck would they do to me? Brother Frederick said the road is only dangerous at night. Hardly soothing news, seeing as it was night.

A TIME BOMB

In a nation of 27 million, at least 5 percent of Kenyans live as squatters, most occupying very small strips of land, rarely wider than 20 feet, on which they build illegal huts. For instance, in Kagoshi, near Mount Kenya, 1,500 people live pretty much in the gutter, along a narrow strip of land adjacent to a road.

The unemployment rate in Kenya is about 45 percent. Farm workers on tea, pineapple and coffee plantations are forced to live on subsistence wages.

Kenya is a time bomb waiting to explode.

Work is more than a way to make a living; it is a form of continuing participation in God's act of creation.... If the dignity of work is to be protected, then the basic rights of workers, owners and managers must be respected—the right to productive work, to decent and fair wages, to organize and join unions, to economic initiative, and to ownership and private property." (The U.S. Catholic Conference Administrative Board, from *Faithful Citizenship: Civic Responsibility for a New Millennium, 2000*)

LIVING WITHOUT

Just from casual conversations with the friars, I am learning a lot about life in Africa. For persons fleeing poverty and starvation, forced migration has become a way of life on this continent. Extremes of famine, war, poverty and draught uproot thousands of Africans. Most migrants end up living as squatters in massive slums in the largest cities, where they endure a life without running water, without toilets,

without electricity, with nothing but misery and diseases, such as malaria and tuberculosis. To be a migrant in Africa is to be a nonperson, unwanted and unneeded.

Turmoil and tragedy are commonplace in Africa. Choice in Africa is often reduced to famine or flood, corruption or coup, cease-fire or peace pact. Africa is slipping out of the control of the leaders who claim to govern it, and beyond the reach of the international institutions and coalitions that seek to rescue it. Africa is suffering from multiple crises: ecological, economic and political. Roads are crumbling and health systems have failed. The phones don't work and power outages are normal. Schoolchildren have neither books nor desks nor teachers. Fresh water and forests are under increasing and unprecedented stress. War and disease thwart any effort to reduce the severe poverty. Real per capita income across the continent is estimated to be under $500. More than 40 percent of Africa's population live on less than a dollar a day. Two hundred million Africans lack access to health facilities. Every year, 2 million African children die before they reach their fifth birthday. And on top of this

woe, AIDS is taking a terrible toil, infecting nearly 21 million people.

What can be done? I think the world should begin by uniting in prayer for Africa.

To clasp the hands in prayer is the beginning of an uprising against the disorder of the world. (Karl Barth, cited in *True Prayer: An Invitation to Christian Spirituality* by Kenneth Leech, page 80)

OUT OF AFRICA

Friday, May 19, 2000—5:30 p.m., Nairobi, Kenya. I have decided to go home to Los Angeles three days early and will be leaving tomorrow.

Why?

Because I have had enough.

Kenya is emotionally and physically exhausting. Nothing works. Nairobi lacks enough water to power the generators that provide electricity, and so officials plan to start rationing the electricity; starting this weekend, the electricity will be cut off for eight to ten hours a day. The phones don't work; I just spent nearly three hours trying to call the airline office. The friars will be busy this weekend, leaving me only Monday to see more slums, and to be honest, I have seen enough. I have already shot twenty-two rolls of film—nearly 900 photographs that captured the harsh reality of life in Nairobi for the thousands of people who live in the sprawling slums that dot the city, where open sewers and disease make life a living hell.

After five full days of witnessing the misery of extreme poverty, famine, drought, hunger, illness, suffering and death, I simply need to go home a few days early. During my time in Kenya, I did not see any wildlife. I have seen only life wildly out of balance, where poverty is crushing people to death in ways too cruel to imagine.

My mind is filled with horrific scenes from the slums I have visited during my week in Africa. The slums are bursting at their seams, an endless maze of mud huts. We would walk all day long and not reach the end of a slum, passing along the way an array of makeshift businesses selling everything from goats to flip-flops to anemic-looking vegetables. Toilets are a rarity and most people use the ground. Electricity and running water are luxuries beyond most people's wildest dreams. And

in this damp, overcrowded environment, every disease imaginable festers and spreads like wildfire. Domestic violence and rape are common. Politicians view the slums as public lands overrun by squatters who are ineligible for basic city services, such as sanitation and garbage removal. Heaps of garbage pile up in every empty space. I am deeply saddened by the unthinkable, unending misery.

I have been reading Evelyn Underhill's *The School of Charity* and this sentence jumped out at me:

> Our whole life is to be poised on a certain glad expectancy of God; taking each moment, incident, choice and opportunity as material placed in our hand by the Creator whose whole intricate and mysterious process moves toward the triumph of the Cross, and who has given each living spirit a tiny part in the vast work of transformation. (Page 108)

Well, I have seen some of the cross these past few months, and I guess it is hard to believe my tiny part in the work of transforming the pain into triumph can make any difference. But I must believe, I

must allow God to work things out according to his mysterious plan.

REALITY BITES

Saturday, May 20, 2000—Nairobi Airport. Shortly after the plane door was closed, the flight attendants announced they would be fumigating the cabin, and they asked all passengers wearing contact lenses to shut their eyes. They then came through the cabin spraying a sickly sweet aerosol spray into the air, in an effort to kill any hitchhiking bugs that entered the plane while the door was open. The white cloud quickly dissipated, leaving behind only a reminder of what the poor live with every day in Africa: fear of infection from mosquitoes. Some of the most common mosquito diseases found in Africa are malaria, dengue fever, yellow fever and encephalitis. The harsh reality of these diseases, whose symptoms include nausea, vomiting, convulsions, comas, hemorrhaging and inflammation of the brain, bites about 300 million poor people a year, mostly in South America and Africa.

A POOR INVESTMENT

Malaria-prone countries have a per capita annual income of less than $500. The big pharmaceutical companies see malaria as a disease of the very poor, and so they consider research and the development of drugs to fight the disease as a poor investment.

THE RICHNESS OF GOD

As the plane climbed through the hot African night air, I leaned back and closed my eyes. The flight from Nairobi, Kenya, to Amsterdam would take eight hours and forty minutes. I took a deep breath, as if to fight off the frustration of spending so much time in such cramped quarters. And then there would be an even longer connecting flight to Los Angeles—ten hours and fifty minutes. As I felt myself becoming frustrated at the prospect of the long, tedious trip home, I suddenly thought of a "home" I had visited in one of Nairobi's many large slums. The home consisted of one room. One small room, measuring no more than fifteen feet by ten feet. The walls were made of mud and sticks. There were no windows. And, of course, no electricity or running water. A few steps outside the front door, an open sewer ran past the house, carrying with it a vile stench.

I believe God has drawn me to the margins of society; I pray some day soon I understand why. I only know I feel the reality of God more strongly in these horrible slums than I do anywhere else.

The spiritual lesson seems clear: to become poor is to know the richness of God. And of course, that does not mean I am endorsing poverty. Far from it. The kind of physical poverty I have been witnessing is an injustice on a grand scale. It must be eliminated; human dignity must be restored.

I need to become poor in spirit, to recognize my own limits and my own dependence upon God for everything.

The only thing I am sure of is my own sinfulness and my profound need of God's love and mercy. And as that awareness grows, I, in turn, have no other choice but to be more merciful and loving to all, especially to those who live at the margins of society.

> Only through poverty of spirit do we draw close to God; only through it does God draw near to us. Poverty of spirit is the meeting place of heaven and earth, the mysterious place where God and we encounter each other, the point where infinite mystery meets concrete existence. (Johannes Metz, *Poverty of Spirit*, page 26)

THE FIRST STEP

The first step toward authentic social justice begins with personal conversion—a continual growth in knowledge, love and service of Christ. We must become less self-absorbed and our lives lived more in communion with the poor. Personal conversion and the common good go hand in hand. Injustice is rooted in sin.

LIGHT AND SHADOWS

When I pick up my camera and look through the viewfinder, I am intensely aware of light and the way shadows emerge in contradistinction to it. In the same manner, I only began to see my own sin through contrast with grace. A photographer must be aware of light and a saint must be aware of his or her flaws and weaknesses. When by grace the light of God's love penetrates my soul, it illuminates my most hidden imperfections. For a long time I ran from the light, taking refuge in things that stroke my ego. Society said sin was a worthless concept from the dark ages. But sin is a reality, even if it is ignored. By God's grace, the dance of light and shadow has shown me that I need to face the Light and the dark shadows of my sin.

PERFECT LOVE

Saint Thérèse of Lisieux said, "My vocation is to love." That is our vocation, too, our daily vocation. Only love will put you on the path to sanctity. Only love will get you to heaven. And your love must include the people who are marginalized, the people who are homeless, the people who are dirty and who smell, the people who are addicted, the people who are imprisoned and the people who live in the squalor of Third World countries. Love must go way beyond ourselves and our family and friends. It must go to all those whom everyone else rejects or excludes. No one should be

outside the perimeter of our love.

This is the only thing that matters: that you have love for one another.

If love is absent from your life, Christ is absent from your life. If you deny your love to someone, you deny your love to Christ. That is how radical the gospel is.

The Eucharist compels us to become what we have received: Perfect Love.

POVERTY OF SPIRIT

Without poverty of spirit, there can be no abundance of God.
—Archbishop Oscar Romero

Poverty of spirit is a manger of gentle receptivity that allows the Divine to be born within us. To be wholly present to God, with all of our heart, mind and soul, we must be poor in spirit.

Poverty of spirit is far more than material poverty. While material poverty may help to facilitate poverty of spirit, it is nonetheless important to realize that a person without possessions can still be possessed by a craving for things. It is the craving that makes us restless, distracting our hearts and

minds from being present to God alone. Poverty of spirit frees us from being divided by false idols and uncurbed passions.

Poverty of spirit does not refer to an economic condition. It reflects the human reality that we are poor before God and we need to depend on God alone for true fulfillment.

We must be on guard not to confuse the necessities of life with what is luxurious. The humble simplicity that embodies poverty of spirit stands in stark contrast with the unbridled pursuit of comfort, power, pleasure and riches that permeates a society prizing possessions as a good in itself.

Poverty of spirit is a means of maintaining a continual attitude of dying to self without succumbing to self-hatred or causing a lack of self-esteem. We need to die to self because it is the only way to be fully alive to God.

THE GIFT OF POVERTY

The life of Saint Francis of Assisi reflected his profound understanding of the Incarnation of Christ, which, for Saint Francis, clearly illustrated the immense generosity of God. God did not cling to divinity; instead, God freely relinquished the limitless power and privilege of divinity and entered the limitations and suffering of the human condition. Through the Incarnation of Christ, God entered into the poor, ordinary life of humans. The majesty and power of the Divine yielded to the simplicity, humility, frailty and poverty of a manger in a stable. Jesus was born poor and lived most of his life in obscurity, without power or fortune.

Saint Francis loved the humanity of Jesus, and came to know his own true humanity and dignity by striving to become like Christ. By entering fully into the Incarnation of God, Saint Francis was able to recognize the divine image within all creation. For Saint Francis, all creation sang the praises of God.

The gift of poverty enables us to share in the Incarnation of Christ. It allows us to empty ourselves of every vestige of pride and power that keeps us from entering fully into a union with God.

ALL OF CREATION

Increasing our love of God goes hand in hand with increasing our love of humans and all of creation.

WHEN DID I SEE YOU NAKED?

I was walking down a busy street in Rome, not far from the main train station, when my full attention was arrested by a disturbing sight. I had been lost in thought as I walked. It was late June of 2001 and I was wrestling with the future of this book. The traveling was over, the photographs taken and the text written. And I had a contract with a publisher in New York City. But poverty still had something more to teach me.

The publisher was not happy with the text of the book. They found some of it to be "offensive" and "exclusionary." A secular publishing house, they wanted the Christian dimension of the book to be toned down. I was coming perilously close to believing that the cumulative effect of all the deletions and revisions I had already had to make at their behest had stripped the book

of its core message. That emerging belief presented me with a challenging dilemma: publish the book or follow the dictates of my conscience and withdraw it.

Books featuring photography are expensive, and landing a publishing contract for a photography book is difficult. The thought of withdrawing the book frightened me. The secular publisher had extensive distribution channels. Publishers who specialize in religious books often have difficulty getting the large book chains to stock their titles. And so placing the book with a secular house had been a big break for me, and I was thrilled to have the chance to get a strong Christian message into the broader marketplace.

But reaching a wider audience was not the reason I wrote the book. I wrote the book to discover the truth and to communicate it. The book was never about "my photography" or "my writing"; it was about the people in the photographs and my pledge to them to tell the story of the plight of the poor. And suddenly, I found myself on the verge of betraying them by not being honest with myself and standing firm for the hard truths I presented in the book. As I walked through the streets of Rome that sunny June day, the storm clouds of indecision raged within me. I saw merits for accepting the changes the publisher required—after all, it would still be a good book and might actually do some good. But, deep within my heart and spirit, I knew the demanding, tough tone of the book needed to be maintained. Jesus' attitude regarding our response to the poor is radical. Jesus is not asking us to give the poor some spare change; he is asking us to give them our lives. And I needed to face this brutal reality: Jesus' teaching, which is almost impossible to follow, had been erased from the book. But I was afraid to withdraw the book.

A few weeks earlier, I thought I had been given a sign from God that I needed to resist the publisher's efforts to soften Jesus' hard message. I was staying in a hotel near Vatican City that catered to Christian pilgrims. Early one morning I went out for a cappuccino. Just outside the gates of the hotel complex, a homeless man was asleep on the ground, bundled up under frayed blankets. At his feet lay a sleeping German shepherd. Sores covered the dog's body.

It was a sad sight.

After having my coffee, I purchased a pastry to give to the man. As I placed it next to him, he stirred. He opened his eyes, startled by my presence. I said, "Here is something to eat."

He said, "Thank you."

I was surprised he spoke English. I guessed he was in his fifties. His bald head was soiled. I could not help contrasting the way we had each spent the night. I had comfort, warmth, a soft bed, a room with a private bath, a bottle of fine Italian chianti and earlier in the evening I had a nice meal with a friend. He slept on the ground with his dog. It was a chilly night. When he got up, his immediate concern would be finding a place to relieve himself. A hot shower and nice cup of hot cappuccino are not options for him.

I said good-bye and walked away. I paused at the gate and looked back at the man on the ground. A young priest, staying at the hotel, walked past the man; the priest was pulling a small, black leather rolling suitcase. He glanced at the man as he walked by, but did not pause.

A little later, I headed out again to go to Mass at St. Peter's. The man was still there. I went up to him and coughed loudly to let him know someone was approaching. He opened his eyes. I saw the unopened bag containing the pastry and said, "Oh, you haven't eaten it yet." He nodded his head no, his eyes squinting from the bright, rising sun. I handed him 2,000 lire—about a buck in U.S. currency. I could see he was shivering. He had on a short-sleeved shirt. I reached down to pull the blanket over him. The dog growled. I said to the man, "What is your name?"

"Michael."

"I'm Gerry."

"Hi."

"Where are you from, Michael?"

"France."

The dog seemed agitated by my presence. His job was to protect Michael. Michael told him to be still, that it was all right.

I reached down and touched Michael on the shoulder and said, "God bless you."

As I walked to Mass, I wondered how Michael got through the night, how he wound up on the ground in Rome, just a short walk from the Vatican.

261

Why do I care?

Why did I write the poverty book?

Did God want me to write it?

Is God asking me to compromise on what he taught me in the slums of the world?

The questions swirled around my mind.

Michael needs help...and a lot more than a pastry and a buck.

At Mass, the book's title reverberated in my mind: *When Did I See You Hungry?*

This morning, Lord.

And all I could do was give you a pastry and a buck.

Was that enough?

I thought this incident was God's way of telling me not to water down the message in my book. My concern cannot be publication...or my own comfort and security. I have been given much and therefore much is required.

But I was afraid to let go of the book. And so the incident with Michael quickly faded from my memory.

But weeks later, another homeless person would jog my memory and help me overcome my fear. Fear keeps us from loving. And the only way to break the bondage of fear is to embrace poverty of spirit, which creates awareness that I need God's forgiveness, mercy and help more than anything else. Poverty of spirit shines a light on a very basic truth: by myself, I am nothing.

As I walked absentmindedly down the busy street in Rome, a homeless woman walked toward me. She was wearing a tattered, soiled T-shirt. And nothing else. She was naked from the waist down, her pubic hairs fully exposed. A blank stare on her face, she seemed oblivious to the people she passed. As she passed me, I turned to continue looking at her. Her rear end was on full display.

But as shocking as the sight was, the reaction from people walking past her was even more disgraceful. I followed her, and was appalled to see teenagers taunting and teasing her, scornfully pointing at her. Many adults, both tourists and citizens of Rome, laughed or giggled. Some raised their eyes skyward and shook their heads in disgust. I saw one nicely dressed woman bless herself as she passed the woman, which was better than laughing at her, but she did not pause to consider how to help. I did not see one ounce of compassion or sympathy. Perhaps everyone was too busy.

The half-naked woman on the crowded streets was ignored or scorned. I knew then why I could not water down my book. The book had been reduced to: "God is love, so be nice when you can to the poor." And that is not good enough.

As I followed the woman, we passed a street vendor's table covered with inexpensive T-shirts. I spotted a pile of light-weight running pants. I purchased a pair. As the nearly naked woman paused at a corner, I got her attention and handed her the pants. She looked at me. She did not say anything, but she knew what I was doing. And she was aware of her state of undress. She took the pants, leaned up against a building and put them on. She looked at me, and while her expression did not really change, I saw in her eyes that she was thankful. She walked away, without uttering a word or turning back.

I cried. I stood and watched as she disappeared into the crowd. I hoped she could walk with a bit more dignity and not have to face the ridicule of being either so poor or so mentally ill that she was reduced to appearing in public half naked.

Her image was burned into my mind.

It would be a few weeks before I was able to stand up for her and Michael and the hundreds of desperately poor people I was graced with the chance to encounter as I wrote this book.

I pulled the book from the New York City publisher and trusted God would help me find another publisher who would not be afraid to publish something more in harmony with my vision for the book. You are holding the fruit of that trust.

In the end, I have no answers to the crippling poverty that imprisons millions of people around the world. All the wonderful programs and services offered by governments and churches will never eradicate the problem. The problem is too vast. The only hope is a fundamental shift in our attitudes toward ourselves and the poor. As a Christian, I think the only effective answer is for the followers of Jesus to attend to his plea that we become one with the poor and put their well-being before our own.

And, believe me, I am not asking you, dear reader, to do that, because I know I am not able to do it. But together we must walk toward that impossible ideal, and the closer we come to reaching it, the closer humanity will come to ending the suffering so many endure every day.

Meanwhile, may God show you what is yours to do...and may God give you the grace to do it.

A FILM

Near the end of 2001, thanks to the generous financial support of a man in San Luis Obispo, California, who had written to me after reading *The Sun and Moon Over Assisi*, I made a short film based on the photos in this book. After public screenings of the film I was confronted with prolonged silence, followed by one desperate question: What do I do?

The film, and the book also, leave people feeling devastated, and they want to know what they could possibly do in the face of such a colossal, global problem.

Father Mychal Judge, O.F.M., was a Franciscan priest and the chaplain of the New York City Fire Department. He was killed on September 11, 2001, while administering last rites to a dying fireman at the foot of the World Trade Center. This was his daily prayer:

> Lord, take me where you want me to go;
> Let me meet who you want me to meet;
> Tell me what you want me to say,
> and
> Keep me out of your way.
>
> ©2001 HOLY NAME PROVINCE

And I have found the following words from Archbishop Oscar Romero helpful when I feel overcome by the scope of the problem of global hunger and think I can't make a difference:

> We cannot do everything and there is a sense of liberation in realizing that. This enables us to do something and to do it very well. It may be incomplete, but it is a beginning, a step along the way, an opportunity for God's grace to enter and do the rest.

This book's message is radical, difficult and demanding. It presents a lofty ideal, a goal for each of us to struggle to reach. And with God's help, we can reach it. Each of us can do more; each of us needs to do more. Do what you can, today and everyday. Pray that you do not forget or ignore the poor and the hungry.

To look at these photographs and not respond in some concrete way is worse than not having seen them at all...because now you know, now you know just how widespread and severe the problem is, now you know it is your duty as a Christian—as a believer in God no matter what faith you follow and as a human being—to do something.

You are about to read what I did last week—and it was not enough. The following was written on November 26, 2001, and is based on an encounter I had with an old, homeless woman.

ALONE ON A CORNER

Yesterday, November 25, 2001, the Catholic Church celebrated the Feast of Christ the King. It was a clear, crisp Sunday. The strong winds and heavy rains on Saturday washed away every trace of smog that usually blankets the San Fernando Valley. As my wife and I drove to Sunday brunch, the mountains encircling the valley were clearly visible beneath the bright blue sky. The sky was dotted with puffy white clouds. It was a perfect day, a day fit for a king. We ate at a nice restaurant in Toluca Lake, a place where you can find Bob Hope's home, but you will not find a lake.

As we pulled out of the restaurant parking lot, I spotted an elderly, homeless woman across the street. She looked cold. She was wearing a heavy coat; a woolen scarf covered her head. She was pacing back and forth in front of her shopping cart, which was filled with what appeared to be all her earthly possessions. I said to my wife, "I see that old lady all the time. That is her corner. Whenever I eat at Mo's, I always see her, and can't help wondering about her."

Kathy said, "Why don't you pull over and we'll give her some money." As I pulled the car to the curb, Kathy pulled a ten-dollar bill from her purse. "You give it to her," she said.

I walked up to the woman and said, "Hi. You look cold."

She gave me a startled look. I guess not many people stop to talk with her. I wondered if she had any mental problems.

Life on the street for the elderly is awfully lonely and it pushes them into deep depression, despair and general craziness. She said, "Yeah, it is getting cold. I guess winter is here."

She seemed lucid. I asked, "Do you need some money?"

I sounded stupid: *No, she doesn't need any money.*

Rather than call attention to my dumb question, she meekly shook her head yes. I handed her the folded bill. When she noticed that it was a ten-dollar bill, her face brightened, revealing a gentle smile. "Thank you," she said.

I got back in the car and we drove away.

A few blocks later, we wondered how she stayed dry during the torrential rains on Saturday. Her clothes looked filthy. I told my wife that the cuffs of her pants were muddied, as if she had waded through puddles of water. Beneath the frayed woolen scarf was a gentle, round face that bore the ravages of a long, hard life. Her corner is in the heart of an upscale neighborhood where you do not often see homeless people. There certainly are no shelters or soup kitchens in the area. We felt as if we wanted to do more for her. We had a fleeting, crazy idea of opening a little storefront place where someone like her could find a little relief from the cold and loneliness of the streets. But we quickly realized how impractical an idea that was for us. Still, she remained on our minds. We did not know what to do for her.

Later that night, Kathy handed me a small bundle of warm clothes, consisting of a sweater and two heavy sweatshirts. She said, "If you see that old lady tomorrow, give her these." What a great idea...and practical, too. She had to need warm clothing.

This morning I drove to her corner. And there she was. She wore the same clothing, and was once again pacing up and down in front of her cart trying to stay warm by constantly moving. I parked the car and walked up to her.

"Hi. Do you remember me? I gave you ten dollars yesterday."

"Oh yes, sure. But it was later in the day."

She was right. She not only remembered me but also knew the time of day when she had last seen me. Again, I could not help but notice how clear-minded she seemed. So many of the long-term homeless slip into a state of dementia; plainly she had not.

I said, "I am glad you remember me. I have been thinking about you, and I thought you might need some warm clothes. Here is a wool sweater and two nice sweatshirts."

I fully expected her to grab them from me. Wrong. "Well, that is very nice of you. But I really don't have room for them." She pointed to her shopping cart, and showed me how full it was. "I don't have much space, and I can't carry any extra stuff because I gotta' always be on the go."

"Are you sure?" I asked, adding, "These are very warm."

"No, I don't have a tent or anyplace to store things. I got all I need. I even have food." She showed me a plastic bag. Inside was a jar of peanut butter and some crackers.

I had taken my camera with me. I was hoping perhaps the woman would allow me to photograph her. I have thousands of photos of people in slums around the world, as well as homeless people in some really bad neighborhoods in cities here in America. But this poor woman lived on a sunny corner in a nice suburb. She lived in my neighborhood. I was thinking about the dramatic contrast the photograph would have. I told her—in as few words as possible—about my travels to the slums of the world and my photo/essay book on global poverty. I asked her how long she had been homeless. But instead of answering, she began to back away, curtly saying, "I'm not here to give interviews."

I apologized, saying I was just trying to learn about the poor and homeless because I want to try to help. I told her I wouldn't ask about her life. "However," I said, "I would like to know your name."

"Dolores. What's your name?"

"Gerry."

She stepped back toward me. I said, "Dolores, as long as I can't give you these clothes, could I give you a little more money?"

"No thanks, Gerry," she said. "You were very generous yesterday, and I appreciated it. I have enough. Give it to someone else who really needs it."

Her answer blew me away. She wasn't crazy, yet it seemed crazy that she would not take the money.

I said good-bye. She gave me a smile and waved.

I went to noon Mass. I was about twenty minutes early. As I sat alone in the empty church, I thought about Dolores. I drove up in my Mercedes and tried to give her what I thought she needed, warm clothes and a few bucks. She has absolutely nothing, yet she said she didn't need anything. She is living day to day, hour to hour, alone on a corner. What she needs is love. I could not give her that. Mass began. The Gospel reading was about the widow's mite, the story in Luke's Gospel in which Jesus saw some rich people putting their money in the temple treasury. After seeing a poor widow put in two small, copper coins, Jesus said that the poor woman gave more than the rich people. Say what, Jesus? The rich gave hefty donations. What do you mean she gave more than them? Jesus explained that the rich gave from their surplus while the widow contributed what she could not afford to give—every penny she had to live on.

In terms of riches, I am to God what Dolores is to me. Actually, the difference between God and me is infinitely greater than the difference between Dolores and me. God wants to give me everything I need. And I tell God I don't need anything, that I can handle it myself.

Slowly, I am waking up to the fact that I need God for absolutely everything, and that without God I am just a lonely, cold man living on a corner near God's infinitely bountiful kingdom.

I tried to give Dolores some spare change and unwanted clothing. Jesus wants me to give her everything I have, wants me to give her my very life. Jesus is not being realistic; he knows I can't give her everything I have. So what is Jesus telling me? Jesus is merely reflecting the unfathomable generosity of his Father. God wants to give us everything.

And what does God want?

Simple, just one thing: our hearts.

But our hearts are taken...taken by thousands of false gods, smitten by countless empty promises.

Dolores stands alone on a corner in Toluca Lake.

What can I do? Nothing, if I think whatever I do I have to do on my own. In the face of such widespread homelessness, I am weak and powerless to do anything. But such thoughts reveal my self-centeredness. I must never forget that I only have to do what I can do and trust God will do the rest.

When I walked out of church after Mass today, a man came up to me and said he needed money to get something to eat. I've seen him before, and I've always walked past him, pretending I had not seen him. But today, I gave him the money Dolores told me to give to someone who needed it more than she did.

Dolores stands alone on a corner in Toluca Lake. Tomorrow, I am going to get her a coffee and stand with her for a while. And maybe someday I will have the faith and generosity of the woman in Luke's Gospel who gave away her two small coins, who gave away all she had, trusting God would give her all she needed.

An old woman in the Gospel of Luke and an old woman on a corner in Toluca Lake came together today to show me just how radical the gospel is. I guess that is why it is so hard for me to follow . . . for if I did, my entire life would radically change. I would have to give God my heart. I pretend I have given my heart to God, but I know I am holding something back, that I am miles away from total surrender, miles away from trusting God for everything, miles away from experiencing God's infinitely bountiful kingdom, a kingdom of truth and life, a kingdom of holiness and grace, a kingdom of justice, love and peace.

The Feast of Christ the King marks the end of the liturgical year. Advent begins in a few days. Fittingly, we end the year by celebrating the majesty and greatness of Christ. But Christ the King is no ordinary king. He never sought worldly power or influence. Christ is a king who wished to liberate not rule. He is the king of surrender, dying on a cross between two prisoners, surrounded in death, as in life, by outcasts and the despised. He is a king crowned with humility and suffering. Jesus entered our weakness and brokenness in order to show us the path to resurrection.

Christ the King, please give me the grace to surrender fully my heart to your Kingship and to walk, as you did, with the poor and the hungry.

THE COLLECTION BASKET

Most of the poor at Santa Catarina de Sena Church in Manaus, Brazil, in the heart of the Amazon region, have no money to place in the collection basket during the offertory of the Mass. But they are still able to give something. I attended Mass there in 2002 and saw that, rather than passing a plate or basket down each pew, two altar servers, both young girls, stood in front of the altar holding wicker baskets. The congregation came forward and placed their offering in the basket. A friend whispered to me that those who have no money to give are invited to come to the altar servers and offer themselves in silent prayer. Many did.

I had no money with me. Still, I walked up to one of the little girls who held a nearly empty basket. Placing my hands palms down over the basket, I offered myself to Jesus. The symbolic gesture so moved me, I began to cry as I walked back to my seat. Offering myself felt better than it would have if I had been able to put $1,000 into the basket. I loved the symbolism of the poor being able to offer something of great value—themselves—when they have no

money. I later learned that after such an offering, people pray that God gives them an opportunity to perform an act of kindness after the liturgy has ended.

The poor around the world have taught me a great deal. Over and over again I have been astounded by their generosity, kindness and mercy to others, more often than not rendered while they themselves were in a state of absolute insufficiency. It is so easy for me to give from my excess, from what I really don't need. But Christ desires that we do much more than simply share our leftovers. I think Christ truly rejoices when he sees a poor woman in Manaus offering herself when she has no money to give. Even those who drop a small coin in the basket are giving out of their want, and perhaps the coin they drop in the basket is the only coin they have. And yet they give it…or give themselves.

Oh Lord, help me be more like the poor I have been privileged to meet while writing this book. And please, Lord, help me always to realize that I am totally dependent on you, no matter how much money I have in my pocket.

STICKBALL

In a few months, I will be celebrating my fifty-fifth birthday. It seems like only yesterday I was a kid playing stickball on the streets of New York City. Life goes by far too fast. And because we have this goofy idea we have endless days before us, life also goes by far too slowly. Life is complex, confounding and contradictory. It is at once beautiful and ugly, wonderful and dreadful. Making sense of life takes a lifetime.

My life has had its share of ups and downs, successes and failures. I made an awful lot of mistakes. I hurt a lot of people, and I've helped a few. In my fifty-five years, I've done a lot of stuff. But today, none of that stuff, none of those accomplishments, means anything to me.

This book represents the first and only time I responded to grace, and grace is the true author of this book. I was merely a humble instrument, struggling to follow where grace took me. Before the first photograph was taken, before the first word was placed on a page, I was skeptical about miracles. Now, as I am about to send the book to the publisher, miracles are an expected part of life.

I could not have completed this book without the help of countless people. Dozens of Franciscan friars and sisters, along with many secular Franciscans, not only escorted me through numerous slums, but they also shared with me the insights they had garnered while serving the poor and tended to all my physical needs, feeding, housing and transporting me while I was in their countries. And there were many generous people who saw me struggling with the heavy financial burden associated with the travel, photography and research and who offered a helping hand that allowed me to continue. I am especially grateful to Patti Normile, who is a secular Franciscan, and her husband Ray for their generous financial support, and to Gregory Morris of San Luis Obispo, California, for his faith shown in funding the film without hesitation. I truly appreciate Martin Sheen's willingness to narrate the film. And I am deeply indebted to the wonderful, dedicated and talented people at St. Anthony Messenger Press who believed in the book and made it better.

I wasn't very good at stickball. And I am not very good at helping the poor or following Christ. It is too late for stickball, but I am going to dedicate myself to doing a better job of embracing the poor and the one true lover of the poor, Jesus Christ, by following the example of Saint Francis of Assisi.

AN AMBASSADOR OF GOD'S PEACE.

I'm tired. I'll stop. And tomorrow, I will do my utmost to be alert to God's grace and the poor person it places in my path. And God's grace will give me the wisdom to know what needs to be done and the strength to do it.

As a secular Franciscan, I would like to leave you with what I consider a perfect ending. And the perfect beginning for living this book's message.

The Prayer Attributed to Saint Francis of Assisi

Fresco of Saint Francis, Assisi, Italy

Lord,

make me an ambassador of your peace.

Where there is hatred, help me foster love.

Where there is injury,

help me bring pardon.

Where there is doubt,

help me foster faith.

Where there is despair,

help me bring hope.

Where there is darkness,

help me shed light.

Where there is sadness,

help me bring joy.

O Divine Master, help me remember

that it is far better for me

to console rather than be consoled;

to understand rather than be understood;

to love rather than be loved.

For it is in giving that we receive;

it is in pardoning that we are pardoned;

and it is in dying that we are born to eternal life.

—ADAPTED BY THE AUTHOR

Bernard of Clairvaux: Selected Works (Classics of Western Spirituality), trans. G. R. Evans. Mahwah, N.J.: Paulist Press, 1988.

Berrigan, Daniel, S.J. *Uncommon Prayer: A Book of Psalms.* New York: Seabury Press, 1978.

Boff, Leonardo. *The Path to Hope.* Maryknoll, N.Y.: Orbis Books, 1993.

Bonhoeffer, Dietrich. *Ethics.* New York: Macmillan Co., 1959.

_____. *Letters and Papers from Prison,* trans. John W. Doberstein. New York: Macmillan Company, 1962.

Buber, Martin. *The Writings of Martin Buber,* ed. Will Herberg. New York: New American Library, 1983.

Burrows, Ruth. *Ascent to Love: The Spiritual Teaching of St. John of the Cross.* Denville, N.J.: Dimension Books, 1992.

_____. *Living Love.* Danville, N.J.: Dimension Books, 1985.

Cabestrero, Teofilo. *Mystic of Liberation.* Maryknoll, N.Y.: Orbis Books, 1981.

Camara, Dom Helder. *Hoping Against All Hope,* trans. Matthew J. O'Connell. Maryknoll, N.Y.: Orbis Books, 1994.

_____. *Sister Earth: Creation, Ecology, and the Spirit.* Hyde Park, N.Y.: New City Press, 1995.

_____. *Through the Gospel with Dom Helder Camara.* Maryknoll, N.Y.: Orbis Books, 1986.

Cantalamessa, Raniero, O.F.M. CAP. *Poverty,* trans. Charles Serignat, O.F.M. CAP. New York: Alba House, 1997.

Cardenal, Ernesto, et al. *Abide in Love.* Maryknoll, N.Y.: Orbis Books, 1995.

Catechism of the Catholic Church for the United States of America. Washington, D.C.: United States Catholic Conference, Inc., 1994.

Chittister, Joan D. *The Rule of Benedict: Insights for the Ages.* New York: Crossroad, 1996.

Chodron, Pema. *Start Where You Are: A Guide to Compassionate Living.* Boston & London: Shambhala Publications, 1994.

Ciszek, Walter J., S.J. *He Leadeth Me.* San Francisco: Ignatius Press, 1973.

Collopy, Michael. *Works of Love Are Works of Peace: Mother Teresa of Calcutta and the Missionaries of Charity.* San Francisco: Ignatius Press, 1996.

Cunningham, Lawrence. *St. Francis of Assisi.* San Francisco: Harper & Row, 1981.

Dalai Lama. *Ethics for the New Millennium: His Holiness the Dalai Lama.* New York: Riverhead Books, 1999.

de Caussade, Jean-Pierre. *The Sacrament of the Present Moment.* San Francisco: HarperSanFrancisco, 1989.

Dhammapada, The, trans. Eknath Easwaran. Tomales, Calif.: Nilgiri Press, 1986.

Dennis, Marie, Renny Golden, Scott Wright. *Oscar Romero: Reflections on His Life and Writings.* Maryknoll, N.Y.: Orbis Books, 2000.

Dickens, Charles. *The Life of Our Lord.* New York: Simon & Schuster, 1999.

Doherty, Catherine de Hueck. *Poustinia: Christian Spirituality of the East for Western Man.* Glasgow: Fontana Books, 1977.

Farrell, Edward. *Free to Be Nothing.* Collegeville, Minn.: The Liturgical Press, 1989.

Fox, Matthew. *Original Blessing.* Santa Fe, N.M.: Bear and Co. Publishing, 1983.

Francis of Assisi, Saint. *Francis of Assisi: Early Documents, 3 Vols.*, ed. Regis J. Armstrong, O.F.M. CAP., J. A. Wayne Hellmann, O.F.M. CONV. and William J. Short, O.F.M. New York: New City Press, 1999, 2000, 2001.

Gutierrez, Gustavo. *Gustavo Gutierrez: Essential Writings*, ed. James B. Nickoloff. Maryknoll, N.Y.: Orbis Books, 1996.

_____. *We Drink from Our Own Wells: The Spiritual Journey of a People.* Maryknoll, N.Y.: Orbis Books, 1985.

Hartmann, Madeline. *The Man Behind the Miracle: The Story of Alfred Boeddeker, O.F.M.* Fort Bragg, Calif.: Lost Coast Press, 2000.

Heschel, Abraham Joshua. *God in Search of Man: A Philosophy of Judaism.* New York: Noonday Press, 1997.

_____. *Man Is Not Alone.* New York: Farrar, Straus and Giroux, 1951.

_____. *The Sabbath.* New York: Noonday Press, 1996.

Hiral, Most Rev. Ange-Marie. *The Revelations of Margaret of Cortona: The Franciscan Magdalene.* St. Bonaventure, N.Y.: The Franciscan Institute Press, 1952.

Ignatius of Loyola, Saint. *The Spiritual Exercises of St. Ignatius*, trans. Anthony Mottola. New York: Doubleday Image Books, 1964.

Iyer, Raghavan Narasimhan. *The Moral and Political Thought of Mahatma Gandhi.* London: Oxford University Press, 1978.

John Paul II. *The Wisdom of John Paul II*, compiled by Nick Bakalar and Richard Balkin. New York: Vintage Books, 2001.

John of the Cross, Saint. *The Collected Works of St. John of the Cross*, trans. Kieran Kavanaugh, O.C.D. and Otilio Rodriquez, O.C.D. Washington, D.C.: ICS Publications, 1973.

King, Martin Luther, Jr. *Letter from Birmingham City Jail.* Philadelphia: American Friends Service Committee, 1963.

Kirvan, John. *God Hunger.* Notre Dame, Ind.: Sorin Books, 1999.

Leech, Kenneth. *True Prayer: An Invitation to Christian Spirituality.* San Francisco: Harper & Row, 1980.

Levinas, Emmanuel. *Difficult Freedom: Essays on Judaism*, trans. Sean Hand. Baltimore: Johns Hopkins University Press, 1990.

Mairs, Nancy. *Ordinary Time: Cycles in Marriage, Faith, and Renewal.* Boston: Beacon Press, 1993.

Merton, Thomas. *Conjectures of a Guilty Bystander.* New York: Doubleday Image Books, 1968.

_____. *New Seeds of Contemplation, Revised Edition*. New York: W. W. Norton & Co., 1974.

_____. *No Man Is an Island*. San Diego, New York, London: Harcourt Brace Jovanovich, 1955.

_____. *The Other Side of the Mountain: The End of the Journey (The Journals of Thomas Merton, Volume 7 1967-1968)*, ed. Patrick Hart. San Francisco: HarperSanFrancisco, 1998.

Metz, Johannes Baptist. *Poverty of Spirit*, trans. John Drury. Mahwah, N.J.: Paulist Press, 1998.

Mother Teresa. *Everything Starts with Prayer: Mother Teresa's Meditations on Spiritual Life for People of All Faiths*, selected and arranged by Anthony Stern, M.D. Ashland, Ore.: White Cloud Press, 1999.

_____. *The Joy in Loving: A Guide to Daily Living with Mother Teresa*, compiled by Jaya Chaliha and Edward Le Joly. New York: Penguin USA, 2000.

Nouwen, Henri J. M. *Our Greatest Gift: A Meditation on Dying and Caring*. New York: HarperCollins, 1994.

_____. *The Way of the Heart: Desert Spirituality and Contemporary Ministry*. San Francisco: HarperSanFrancisco, 1991.

_____. *With Open Hands*. Notre Dame, Ind.: Ave Maria Press, 1972.

Philokalia, The. London: Faber and Faber, 1979.

Piehl, Mel. *Breaking Bread: The Catholic Worker and the Origin of Catholic Radicalism in America*. Philadelphia: Temple University Press, 1982.

Rinpoche, Tulku Thondup. *The Healing Power of Mind: Simple Meditation Exercises for Health, Well-Being and Enlightenment*. Boston and London: Shambhala Publications, Inc., 1996.

Romero, Archbishop Oscar. *The Violence of Love*, trans. James R. Brockman. Plough Publishing House, 1998.

Russell, Bertrand. *Principles of Social Reconstruction*. London: Routledge, 1997.

Schut, Michael, ed. *Simpler Living, Compassionate Life: A Christian Perspective*. Denver, Col.: Living the Good News, a division of the Morehouse Group, 1999.

Seneca, Lucius Annaeus. *Letters from a Stoic: Epistulae Morales Ad Lucilium (The Penguin Classics L210)*. New York: Viking Press, 1989.

Singh, Sundar. *Wisdom of the Sadhu*. Farmington, Penn.: Plough Publishing House, 2000.

Soelle, Dorothee. *Suffering*, trans. Everett R. Kalin. Philadelphia: Fortress Press, 1975.

Stein, Edith. *Selected Writings of Edith Stein*, trans. and ed. Hilda C. Graef. London: Peter Owen Ltd., 1956.

Thick Nhat Hanh. *The Raft Is Not the Shore*, with Daniel Berrigan, S.J. Maryknoll, N.Y.: Orbis Books, 2001.

Thomas à Kempis. *The Imitation of Christ in Four Books: A Translation from the Latin (Vintage Spiritual Classics)*. New York: Vintage Books, 1998.

Tolstoy, Leo. *A Calendar of Wisdom: Daily Thoughts to Nourish the Soul, Written and Selected from the World's Sacred Texts*, trans. Peter Sekirin. New York: Scribner, 1997.

Vanier, Jean. *Followers of Jesus*. Dublin: Gill and Macmillan Ltd., 1976.

van Ruusbroec, Jan. *The Spiritual Espousals and Other Works*, trans. James A. Wiseman, O.S.B. Mahwah, N.J.: Paulist Press, 1985.

Vatican Council II: The Conciliar and Post Conciliar Documents, ed. Austin Flannery, O.P. Northport, N.Y.: Costello Publishing Company, 1988.

Weil, Simone. *First and Last Notebooks*, trans. Richard Rees. London: Oxford University Press, 1970.

_____. *Two Moral Essays*, trans. Richard Rees. Wallingford, Penn.: Pendle Hill Pamphlet 240, 1981.

• A portion of the author's royalties are being donated to The San Damiano Foundation, which was formed by the author to produce films that showcase the spirituality of Saints Francis and Clare of Assisi, along with the Franciscan concern for social justice, peace and nonviolence. The Foundation has produced a film narrated by Martin Sheen based on this book.

For information about The San Damiano Foundation, write to PO Box 1794, Burbank, CA 91507, or visit their Web site at www.SanDamianoFoundation.org.